THE POCKET
ENQUIRE WITHIN

The Pocket Enquire Within

A guide to the niceties and necessities of Victorian domestic life

Edited by
George Armstrong

Enquirers are referred to the index

BOOKS

Published by Random House Books 2010

2 4 6 8 10 9 7 5 3 1

Introduction copyright © George Armstrong 2010

George Armstrong has asserted his right under the Copyright,
Designs and Patents Act, 1988, to be identified as the author of this work

This edited text is drawn from *Enquire Within Upon Everything*, first
published in Great Britain in 1856 by Houlston and Stoneman

Random House, 20 Vauxhall Bridge Road,
London SW1V 2SA

www.rbooks.co.uk

Addresses for companies within The Random House Group Limited can be
found at: www.randomhouse.co.uk/offices.htm

The Random House Group Limited Reg. No. 954009

A CIP catalogue record for this book is available
from the British Library

ISBN 9781847945846

The Random House Group Limited supports The Forest Stewardship
Council (FSC), the leading international forest certification organisation.
All our titles that are printed on Greenpeace approved FSC certified paper
carry the FSC logo. Our paper procurement policy can be found at
www.rbooks.co.uk/environment

Typeset by SX Composing DTP, Rayleigh, Essex
Printed and bound in Great Britain by
Clays Ltd, St Ives plc

Contents

Introduction

'**WHEN I FIRST BEGAN** tinkering with a software pro-
gramme that eventually gave rise to the idea of the
World Wide Web, I named it ENQUIRE, short for
ENQUIRE WITHIN UPON EVERYTHING, a musty old book of Victorian
advice I noticed as a child in my parents' house . . . With its title
suggestive of magic, the book served as a portal to a world of information, everything from how to remove stains to tips on investing
money. Not a perfect analogy for the Web, but a primitive starting point.'

This was Tim Berners-Lee, talking about his innovative concept of
something we now almost take for granted – the Internet.

ENQUIRE WITHIN UPON EVERYTHING was first published in 1856
by Houlston and Sons of Paternoster Square. It reprinted continuously
and sold millions of copies, 'a sale which the Publishers believe to be
absolutely without precedent among similar works of reference', as the
anonymous editor wrote in the Preface of the seventy-fifth edition in
1890.

'Its prominent characteristics – varied usefulness and cheapness –'
he went on to say, 'have won for it universal esteem. There is scarcely
a spot reached by English civilization to which this book has not found
its way, receiving everywhere the most cordial welcome and winning
the warmest praise.'

This new Pocket Edition includes tips on how to trap snails as well
as hints for husbands. There are recipes for plain pea soup and calf's
head pie, but seekers of advice on the ramifications of letting lodgings
to an immodest woman will be disappointed.

I have retained the instructions on how to make a leech barometer,
but, for reasons of health and safety, Victorian First Aid has been
ruthlessly expunged. On the other hand, there is much to learn about
etiquette, pronunciation, exercise and how to detect copper in pickles or
green tea. *The Pocket Enquire Within* is a glorious hotchpotch of information that reminds us very precisely that the past is another country.
A visit there is both instructive and a source of some merriment.

George Armstrong, London, 2010

Original Preface

IF THERE BE ANY AMONG MY READERS, who, having turned over the pages of "ENQUIRE WITHIN", have hastily pronounced them to be confused and ill-arranged, let them at once refer to THE INDEX, or for ever hold their peace.

The INDEX is, to the vast congregation of useful hints and receipts that fill the boundary of this volume, like the DIRECTORY to the great aggregation of houses and people in London.

No one, being a stranger to London, would run about asking for "MR. SMITH." But, remembering the Christian name, and the profession of the individual wanted, would turn to the DIRECTORY, and trace him out.

Like a house, every paragraph in "ENQUIRE WITHIN", has its number, – and the INDEX is the DIRECTORY which will explain what Facts, Hints, and Instructions *inhabit* that number.

For, if it be not a misnomer, we are prompted to say, that "ENQUIRE WITHIN" is *peopled* with thousands of ladies and gentlemen, who have approved of the plan of the work, and contributed something to its store of useful information. There they are, waiting to be questioned, and ready to reply. Only a short time ago, the facts and information, now assuming the conventional forms of printing types, were active thoughts in the minds of many people. Their fingers traced those thoughts upon the page, for the benefit of whomsoever might need information. We must not separate the thought from the mind which gave it birth; we must not look upon these writings as we should upon the traces left by the snail upon the green leaf, having neither form nor meaning. Behind each page some one lives to answer for the correctness of the information imparted, just as certainly as where, in the window of a dwelling, you see a paper directing you to "ENQUIRE WITHIN", some one is there to answer you.

Old Dr. KITCHENER lives at No. 41; Mrs. HITCHING lives at 161; Mrs. CHILD lives at 203; Dr. BREWER lives at 291; Dr. STENHOUSE at 320; Dr. BURGESS at 324; Dr. ERASMUS WILSON at 399; Dr. SOUTHWOOD SMITH at 401; Dr. BLAIR at 446; M. SOYER at 765; Dr. BABINGTON at 1287; Dr. CLARKE at 1291; Dr. SCOTT, at 1296; the gentleman who lives at 343, has requested us (because of the delicacy of the communication), not to publish his name; a DOCTOR lives at 906; a GARDENER at 1021; a SCHOOLMASTER at 1323; a DANCING MASTER at 1678; an ARTIST at 1851; a NATURALIST at 1925; a MODELLER at 1931; a COOK at 1972; a PHILANTHROPIST at 2006; a LAWYER at 2047; A SURGEON at 2186; a CHESS PLAYER at 2354; a CHEMIST at 2387; a BREWER at 2559; and so on.

Well! there they live – always at home – knock at their doors – ENQUIRE WITHIN, NO FEES TO PAY!!

We have taken so much care in selecting our information, and have been aided by so many kind friends in the production of our volume, that we cannot turn to any page without at once being reminded of the GENEROUS FRIEND WHO ABIDES THERE.

To some extent, though in a far less degree, we have been indebted to the authors of the following useful books. In the first place we must express our chief obligations to "Dr. KITCHENER'S COOK'S ORACLE," to "THE COOK" in "*Houlston and Stoneman's Industrial Library;*" to "THE SHOPKEEPER'S GUIDE," to "Mrs. RUNDELL'S COOKERY," to "HOME TRUTHS, FOR HOME PEACE," and also to "THE FAMILY FRIEND," "TREASURES IN NEEDLEWORK," "THE PRACTICAL HOUSEWIFE," and to "THE FAMILY TREASURY." We now invite the thousands who may "ENQUIRE WITHIN" to our future monthly INTERVIEW, wherein we will endeavour to supply whatever ENQUIRERS may not find by ENQUIRING WITHIN. Our INTERVIEWS will be varied, genial, and original in their arrangement. "*The pleasure of your company is earnestly solicited.*"

Family Life

LOVE'S TELEGRAPH – If a gentleman wants a wife, he wears a ring on the *first* finger of the left hand; if he is engaged, he wears it on the *second* finger; if married on the *third*; and on the fourth if he never intends to be married. When a lady is not engaged, she wears a hoop or diamond on her *first* finger; if engaged, on the *second*; if married, on the *third*; and on the fourth if she intends to die a maid. When a gentleman presents a fan, flower, or trinket, to a lady with the *left* hand, this, on his part, is an overture of regard; should she receive it with the *left* hand, it is considered as an acceptance of his esteem; but if with the *right* hand, it is a refusal of the offer. Thus, by a few simple tokens, explained by rule, the passion of love is expressed: and, through the medium of the telegraph, the most timid and diffident man may, without difficulty, communicate his sentiments of regard to a lady, and, in case his offer should be refused, avoid experiencing the mortification of an explicit refusal.

WEDDING RINGS – The custom of wearing wedding rings, appears to have taken its rise among the Romans. Before the celebration of their nuptials, there was a meeting of friends at the house of the lady's father, to settle articles of the marriage contract, when it was agreed that the dowry should be paid down on the wedding-day or soon after. On this occasion there was commonly a feast, at the conclusion of which the man gave to the woman, as a pledge, a ring, which she put on the fourth finger of her left hand, *because it was believed that a nerve reached thence to the heart*, and a day was then named for the marriage.

ARRANGEMENTS OF THE WEDDING DAY – Wealthy people occasionally marry with *Special Licences*. Special licences are dispensations from the ordinary rule, under which marriages can only take place canonically in the parish church, or other places duly licensed for that purpose. They can only be obtained from the metropolitan or archbishop of the province, and often with no small difficulty, not being readily granted; and when obtained the fees are about £50.

COMMON LICENCES enable persons of full age, or minors with consent of parents or guardians, to be married in the church of the parish in which one of them has resided for three weeks. They are procured from Doctors' Commons, or from any surrogate, at the cost of about £2. 10s.

BANNS must be published *three times* in the parish church, in *each place* where the persons concerned reside. The clerk is applied to on such occasions; his fee is 1s. 6d. When the marriage ceremony is over, the parties repair to the vestry, and enter their names in the parish registry. The registry is signed by the clergyman, and the witnesses present, and a certificate of the registry is given to the bridegroom. There is no charge for the certificate; and the clergyman's fee varies according to circumstances. The clerk will at all times give information thereupon; and it is best for a friend of the bridegroom to attend to the pecuniary settlements.

MARRIAGE BY REGISTRATION – An Act was passed in the reign of William the Fourth, by which it was rendered legal for persons wishing to be married by a civil ceremony, to give notice of their intention to the Registrar of Marriages in their district or districts. Three weeks' notice is necessary, to give which the parties call, separately or together, at the office of the registrar, who enters their names in a book. When the time of notice has expired, it is only necessary to give the registrar an intimation on the previous day, of your intention to attend at his office on the next day, and complete the registration. The ceremony consists of merely answering a few questions, and making the declaration that you take each other to live as husband and wife. The fee amounts only to a few shillings, and in this form no wedding ring is required, though it is usually placed on in the presence of the persons assembled. The married couple receive a certificate of marriage, which is in every respect lawful.

WEDDING DRESS – It is impossible to lay down specific rules for dress, as fashions change, and tastes differ. The great art consists in selecting the style of dress most becoming to the person. A stout person should adopt a different style from a thin person; a tall one from a short one. Peculiarities of complexion, and form of face and figure, should be duly regarded; and in these matters there is no better course than to call in the aid of any respectable milliner and dress-maker, who will be found ready to give the best advice. The bridegroom should simply appear in full dress, and should avoid everything eccentric and broad in style. The bridesmaids should always be made aware of the bride's dress before they choose their own, which should be determined by a proper harmony with the former.

THE ORDER OF GOING TO CHURCH is as follows: – *the bride*, accompanied by her *father*, not unfrequently her *mother*, and uniformly by a *bridesmaid*, occupies the *first carriage*. The father hands out the bride, and leads her to the altar, the mother and bridesmaid following. After them come the other bridesmaids, attended by the groomsmen, if there are more than one.

THE BRIDEGROOM occupies the *last carriage* with the principal groomsman, an intimate friend, or brother. He follows, and stands facing the altar, with *the bride at his left hand*. The father places himself behind, with the mother, if she attends.

THE CHIEF BRIDESMAID occupies a place on the *left* of the *bride*, to hold her gloves, and handkerchief, and flowers; her *companions* range themselves *on the left*. If any difficulties occur from forgetfulness, the vestry-woman can set everything right.

REMEMBER TO *take the licence and the ring with you*. The fee to a clergyman is according to the rank and fortune of the bridegroom; the clerk expects *five shillings*, and a trifle should be given to the vestry-woman or sexton.

WHEN THE CEREMONY IS CONCLUDED, *the bride, taking the bridegroom's arm, goes into the vestry, the others following;* signatures are then affixed, and a registration made, after which the married pair enter their carriage, and proceed to the breakfast, every one else following.

THE ORDER OF RETURN FROM CHURCH differs from the above only in the fact that the bride and bridegroom now ride together, the bride being on his left, and a bridesmaid, and a groomsman, or the father of the bride, occupying the front seats of the carriage.

THE WEDDING BREAKFAST having been already prepared, the wedding party return thereto. If a large party, the bride and bridegroom occupy seats in the centre of the long table, and the two extremities should be presided over by elderly relatives, if possible one from each family. Everybody should endeavour to make the occasion as happy as possible. One of the senior members of either the bride or bridegroom's family, should, some time before the breakfast has terminated, rise, and in a brief but graceful manner, propose the "Health and happiness of the wedded pair." It is much better to drink their healths together than separately; and, after a brief interval, the bridegroom should return thanks, which he may do without hesitation, since no one looks for a speech upon such an occasion. A few words, feelingly expressed, are all that is required. The breakfast generally concludes with the departure of the happy pair upon their wedding tour.

CARDS – With regard to sending out cards, as wedding tours are more extended than in olden times, they are generally forwarded about a week or two previous to the return of the travellers. Plain silver-edged cards are now most fashionable, but questions relative to them ought to be referred to the engraver, as fashions change continually.

RECEPTION – When the married pair have returned, and the day of reception arrives, wedding-cake and wine are handed round, of which every one partakes, and each expresses some kindly wish for the newly married couple. The bride ought not to receive visitors without a mother or sister, or some friend being present, not even if her husband is at home. Gentlemen who are in professions, or have government appointments, cannot always await the arrival of visitors; when such is the case, some old friend of the family should represent him, and proffer an apology for his absence.

THE WEDDING TOUR must depend upon the tastes and circumstances of the married couple. Home-loving Englishmen and women may find much to admire and enjoy without ranging abroad. Those whose time is somewhat restricted, we recommend to sojourn at Tunbridge Wells – Mount Ephraim is especially to be selected – and from thence the most delightful excursions may be made to different parts of the country; those who like sketching, botanising, and collecting sea-weeds, will find ample opportunities for each; those who like old ruins and time-hallowed places may reach them without difficulty. Dover, Canterbury, Folkestone, and Tatwood Castle are all within reach, and what places are more deeply interesting, not only in respect of scenery, but historic associations.

NORTH WALES OFFERS A DELIGHTFUL EXCURSION; the lakes of Westmoreland and Cumberland also; with the magnificent scenery of the Scottish lakes and the Cave of Fingal.

TO THOSE WHO WISH FOR A WIDER RANGE, France, Germany, Switzerland, and the Rhine offer charms which cannot be surpassed.

WEDDING CAKES – Four pounds of fine flour, well dried, four pounds of fresh butter, two pounds of loaf sugar, a quarter of a pound of mace pounded and sifted fine, the same of nut-megs. To every pound of flour add eight eggs; wash four pounds of currants, let them be well picked and dried before the fire; blanch a pound of sweet almonds, and cut them lengthwise very thin; a pound of citron, one pound of candied orange, the same of candied lemon; half a pint of brandy. When these are made ready work the butter with your hand to a cream, then beat in your sugar a quarter of an hour, beat the whites of your eggs to a very strong froth, mix them with your sugar and butter; beat your yolks half an hour at least, and mix them with your cake; then put in your flour, mace, and nutmeg, keep beating it well till your oven is ready – pour in the brandy, and beat the currants and almonds lightly in. Tie three sheets of white paper round the bottom of your hoop to keep it from running out, rub it well with butter, put in your cake, lay the sweetmeats in layers, with cake between each layer, and after it is risen and coloured cover it with paper before your oven is stopped up; it will require three hours to bake properly.

ALMOND ICEING FOR WEDDING CAKE – Beat the whites of three eggs to a strong froth, beat a pound of Jordan almonds very fine with rose water, mix them, with the eggs, lightly together; put in by degrees a pound of common loaf-sugar in powder. When the cake is baked enough, take it out, and lay on the iceing; then put it in to brown.

SUGAR ICEING FOR WEDDING CAKE – Beat two pounds of double-refined sugar with two ounces of fine starch, sift the whole through a gauze sieve, then beat the whites of five eggs with a knife upon a pewter dish for half an hour; beat in your sugar a little at a time, or it will make the eggs fall, and injure the colour; when all the sugar is put in, beat it half an hour longer, and then lay on your almond iceing, spreading it even with a knife. If put on as soon as the cake comes out of the oven it will harden by the time the cake is cold.

ETIQUETTE OF THE NEWLY MARRIED – A newly married couple send out cards immediately after the ceremony to their friends and acquaintance, who, on their part, return either notes or cards of congratulation on the event. As soon as the lady is settled in her new home, she may expect the calls of her acquaintance; for which it is not absolutely necessary to remain at home, although politeness requires that they should be returned as soon as possible. But, having performed this, any further intercourse may be avoided (where it is deemed necessary) by a polite refusal of invitations. Where cards are to be left, the number must be determined according to the various members of which the family called upon is composed. For instance, where there are the mother, aunt, and daughters (the latter having been introduced to society), three cards should be left.

HOW TO TREAT A WIFE – First, get a wife; secondly, be patient. You may have great trials and perplexities in your business with the world, but do not carry to your home a clouded or contracted brow. Your wife may have many trials, which, though of less magnitude, may have been as hard to bear. A kind, conciliating word, a tender look, will do wonders in chasing from her brow all clouds of gloom. You encounter your difficulties in the open air, fanned by heaven's cool breezes; but your wife is often shut in from these healthful influences, and her health fails, and her spirits lose their elasticity. But oh! bear with her; she has trials and sorrows to which you are a stranger, but which your tenderness can deprive of all their anguish. Notice kindly her little attentions and efforts to promote your comfort. Do not treat her with indifference, if you would not sear and palsy her heart, which, watered by kindness, would, to the latest day of your existence, throb with sincere and constant affection. Sometimes yield your wishes to hers. She has preferences as strong as you, and it may be just as trying to yield her choice as to you. Do you find it hard to yield sometimes? Think you it is not difficult for her to give up always? If you never yield to her wishes, there is danger that she will think you are selfish, and care only for yourself, and with such feelings she cannot love as she might. Again, show yourself manly, so that your wife can look up at you and feel that you will act nobly, and that she can confide in your judgment.

HUSBAND AND WIFE – Being hints to each other for the good of both, as actually delivered at our own table:–

HINTS FOR WIVES – If your husband occasionally looks a little troubled when he comes home, do not say to him, with an alarmed countenance, "What ails you, my dear?" Don't bother him; he will tell you of his own accord, if need be. Don't rattle a hailstorm of fun about his ears either; be observant and quiet. Don't suppose whenever he is silent and thoughtful that you are of course the cause. Let him alone until he is inclined to talk; take up your book or your needlework (pleasantly, cheerfully; no pouting – no sullenness), and wait until he is inclined to be sociable. Don't let him ever find a shirt-button missing. A shirt-button being off a collar or wrist-band has frequently produced the first hurricane in married life. Men's shirt-collars never fit exactly – see that your husband's are made as well as possible, and then, if he does fret a little about them, never mind it; men have a prescriptive right to fret about shirt-collars.

HINTS FOR HUSBANDS – If your wife complains that young ladies "now-a-day" are very forward, don't accuse her of jealousy. A little concern on her part only proves her love for you, and you may enjoy your triumph without saying a word. Don't evince your weakness either, by complaining of every trifling neglect. What though her chair is not set so close to yours as it used to be, or though her knitting and crochet seem to absorb too large a share of her attention, depend upon it that, as her eyes watch the intertwinings of the threads, and the manoeuvres of the needles as they dance in compliance to her delicate fingers, she is thinking of courting days, love-letters, smiles, tears, suspicions, and reconciliations, by which your two hearts became entwined together in the network of love, whose meshes you can neither of you unravel or escape.

HINTS FOR WIVES – Never complain that your husband pores too much over the newspaper, to the exclusion of that pleasing converse which you formerly enjoyed with him. Don't hide the paper; don't give it to the children to tear; don't be sulky when the boy leaves it at the door; but take it in pleasantly, and lay it down before your spouse. Think what man would be without a newspaper; treat it as a great agent in the work of civilisation, which it assuredly is; and think how much good newspapers have done by exposing bad husbands and bad wives, by giving their errors to the eye of the public. But manage you in this way: when your husband is absent, instead of gossipping with neighbours, or looking into shop windows, sit down quietly, and look over that paper; run your eye over its home and foreign news; glance rapidly at the accidents and casualties; carefully scan the leading articles; and at tea-time, when your husband again takes up the paper, say, "My dear, what an awful state of things there seems to be in India;" or "what a terrible calamity at the Glasgow theatre;" or "trade appears to be flourishing in the north!" and depend upon it down will go the paper. If he has not read the information, he will hear it all from your lips, and when you have done, he will ask, "Did you, my dear, read Simpson's letter upon the discovery of chloroform?" And whether you did or not, you will gradually get into as cosy a chat as you ever enjoyed; and you will soon discover that, rightly used, the newspaper is the wife's real friend, for it keeps the husband at home, and supplies capital topics for every-day table-talk.

HINTS FOR HUSBANDS – You can hardly imagine how refreshing it is to occasionally call up the recollection of your courting days. How tediously the hours rolled away prior to the appointed time of meeting; how swift they seemed to fly, when met; how fond was the first greeting; how tender the last embrace; how fervent were your vows; how vivid your dreams of future happiness, when, returning to your home, you felt yourself secure in the confessed love of the object of your warm affections. Is your dream realised? – are you so happy as you expected? Why not? Consider whether as a husband you are as fervent and constant as you were when a lover. Remember that the wife's claims to your unremitting regard – great before marriage, are now exalted to a much higher degree. She has left the world for you – the home of her childhood, the fireside of her parents, their watchful care and sweet intercourse have all been yielded up for you. Look then most jealously upon all that may tend to attract you from home, and to weaken that union upon which your temporal happiness mainly depends; and believe that in the solemn relationship of husband is to be found one of the best guarantees for man's honour and happiness.

HINTS FOR WIVES – Perchance you think that your husband's disposition is much changed; that he is no longer the sweet-tempered, ardent lover he used to be. This may be a mistake. Consider his struggles with the world – his everlasting race with the busy competition of trade. What is it makes him so eager in the pursuit of gain – so energetic by day, so sleepless by night – but his love of home, wife, and children, and a dread that their respectability, according to the light in which he has conceived it, may be encroached upon by the strife of existence. This is the true secret of that silent care which preys upon the hearts of many men; and true it is, that when love is least apparent, it is nevertheless the active principle which animates the heart, though fears and disappoint-ments make up a cloud which obscures the warmer element. As above the clouds there is glorious sunshine, while below are showers and gloom, so with the conduct of man – behind the gloom of anxiety is a bright fountain of high and noble feeling. Think of this in those moments when clouds seem to lower upon your domestic peace, and, by tempering your conduct accordingly, the gloom will soon pass away, and warmth and brightness take its place.

HINTS FOR HUSBANDS – Summer is the season of love! Happy birds mate, and sing among the trees; fishes dart athwart the running streams, and leap from their element in resistless ecstasy; cattle group in peaceful nooks, by cooling streams; even the flowers seem to love as they twine their tender arms around each other, and throw their wild tresses about in beautiful profusion; the happy swain sits with his loved and loving mistress beneath the sheltering oak, whose arms spread out, as if to shield and sanctify their pure attachment. What shall the husband do now, when earth and heaven seem to meet in happy union? Must he still pore over the calculations of the counting-house, or ceaselessly pursue the toils of the work-room – sparing no moment to taste the joys which Heaven measures out so liberally? No! "Come, dear wife, let us once more breathe the fresh air of heaven, and look upon the beauties of earth. The summers are few we may dwell together; we will not give them all to Mammon. Again let our hearts glow with emotions of renewed love – our feet shall again tread the green sward, and the music of the rustling trees shall mingle in our whisperings of love!"

HINTS FOR WIVES – "It was!" "It was not!" "It *was!*" "It was *not!*" "Ah!" "Ha!" – Now who's the wiser or the better for this contention for the last word? Does obstinacy establish superiority, or elicit truth? Decidedly not! Woman has always been described as clamouring for the last word: actors, authors, preachers, and philosophers, have agreed in attributing this trait to her, and in censuring her for it. Yet why they should condemn her, unless they wish the matter reversed, and thus committed themselves to the error imputed to her, it were difficult to discover. However, so it is; - and it remains for some one of the sex, by an exhibition of noble example, to aid in sweeping away the unpleasant imputation. The wife who will establish the rule of allowing her husband to have the last word, will achieve for herself and her sex a great moral victory! Is he *right*? – it were a great error to oppose him. Is he *wrong*? – he will soon discover it, and applaud the self-command which bore unvexed his pertinacity. And gradually there will spring up such a happy fusion of feelings and ideas, that there will be no "last word" to contend about – but a steady and unruffled flow of generous sentiment.

A WIFE'S POWER – The power of a wife for good or evil, is irresistible. Home must be the seat of happiness, or it must be for ever unknown. A good wife is to a man, wisdom, and courage, and strength, and endurance. A bad one is confusion, weakness, discomfiture, and despair. No condition is hopeless where the wife possesses firmness, decision, and economy. There is no outward prosperity which can counteract indolence, extravagance, and folly at home. No spirit can long endure bad domestic influence. Man is strong, but his heart is not adamant. He delights in enterprise and action; but to sustain him he needs a tranquil mind, and a whole heart. He needs his moral force in the conflicts of the world. To recover his equanimity and composure, home must be to him a place of repose, of peace, of cheerfulness, of comfort; and his soul renews its strength again, and goes forth with fresh vigour to encounter the labour and troubles of life. But if at home he finds no rest, and is there met with bad temper, sullenness, or gloom, or is assailed by discontent or complaint, hope vanishes, and he sinks into despair.

COUNSELS FOR THE YOUNG – Never be cast down by trifles. If a spider break his thread twenty times, twenty times will he mend it again. Make up your minds to do a thing and you will do it. Fear not if a trouble comes upon you; keep up your spirits, though the day be a dark one. If the sun is going down, look up to the stars. If the earth is dark, keep your eye on Heaven! With God's promises, a man or a child may be cheerful. Mind what you run after! Never be content with a bubble that will burst, firewood that will end in smoke and darkness. Get that which you can keep, and which is worth keeping. Fight hard against a hasty temper. Anger will come, but resist it strongly. A fit of passion may give you cause to mourn all the days of your life. Never revenge an injury. If you have an enemy, act kindly to him and make him your friend. You may not win him over at once, but try again. Let one kindness be followed by another, till you have compassed your end. By little and little, great things are completed; and repeated kindness will soften the heart of stone. Whatever you do, do it willingly. A boy that is whipped to school never learns his lessons well. A man who is compelled to work cares not how badly it is performed. He that pulls off his coat cheerfully, strips up his sleeves in earnest, and sings while he works, is the man of action.

CHILDREN – Happy indeed is the child who, during the first period of its existence, is fed upon no other aliment than the milk of its mother, or that of a healthy nurse. If other food becomes necessary before the child has acquired teeth, it ought to be of a liquid form: for instance, biscuits or stale bread boiled in an equal mixture of milk and water, to the consistence of a thick soup; but by no means even this in the first week of its life.

FLOUR OR MEAL ought never to be used for soup, as it produces viscid humours, instead of a wholesome nutritious chyle.

AFTER THE FIRST SIX MONTHS, weak veal or chicken broth may be given, and also, progressively, vegetables that are not very flatulent; for instance, carrots, endive, spinach, parsnips, with broth and boiled fruit, such as apples, pears, plums, and cherries.

WHEN THE INFANT IS WEANED, and has acquired its proper teeth, it is advisable to let it have small portions of meat, and other vegetables, as well as dishes prepared of flour, &c., so that it may gradually become accustomed to every kind of strong and wholesome food.

WE OUGHT, however, to be cautious, and not upon any account to allow a child pastry, confectionery, cheese, heavy dishes made of boiled or baked flours, onions, horse-radish, mustard, smoked and salted meat, especially pork, and all compound dishes; for the most simple food is the most salubrious.

THE TIME OF TAKING FOOD is not a matter of indifference: very young infants make an exception; for, as their consumption of vital power is more rapid, they may be more frequently indulged with aliment.

IT IS, HOWEVER, advisable to accustom even them to a certain regularity, so as to allow them their victuals at stated periods of the day; for it has been observed, that those children which were fed indiscriminately through the whole day, were subject to debility and disease. The stomach should be allowed to recover its tone, and to collect the juices necessary for digestion, before it is supplied with a new portion of food.

THE FOLLOWING ORDER OF GIVING FOOD to children has been found proper, and conducive to their health: – After rising in the morning, suppose about six o'clock, a moderate portion of lukewarm milk, with well baked bread, which should by no means be new; at nine o'clock, bread with some fruit, or, if fruit be scarce, a small quantity of fresh butter; about twelve o'clock, the dinner of a sufficient quantity; between four and five o'clock, some bread with fruit, or, in winter, the jam of plums, as a substitute for fruit.

ON THIS OCCASION, children should be allowed to eat till they are satisfied, without surfeiting themselves, that they may not crave for a heavy supper, which disturbs their rest, and is productive of bad humours: lastly, about seven o'clock, they may be permitted a light supper, consisting either of milk, soup, fruit, or boiled vegetables and the like, but neither meat nor mealy dishes, nor any article of food which produces flatulency; in short, they ought to eat but little, and remain awake at least for one hour after it.

IT HAS OFTEN BEEN CONTENDED that bread is hurtful to children; but this applies only to new bread, or such as is not sufficiently baked; for instance our rolls, muffins, and crumpets, than which nothing can be more hurtful and oppressive. Good wheaten bread is extremely proper during the first years of infancy; but that made of rye, or a mixture of wheat and rye, would be more conducive to health after the age of childhood.

WITH RESPECT TO DRINK, physicians are decidedly against giving it to children in large quantities, and at irregular periods, whether it consists of the mother's milk, or any other equally mild liquor.

IT IS IMPROPER AND PERNICIOUS
to keep infants continually at the breast;
and it would be less hurtful, nay even
judicious, to let them cry for a few
nights, rather than to fill them
incessantly with milk, which readily
turns sour on the stomach, weakens
the digestive organs, and ultimately
generates scrofulous affections.

IN THE LATTER PART OF THE FIRST YEAR,
pure water may be occasionally given; and if this cannot be procured,
a light and well-fermented table-beer might be substituted. Those
parents who accustom their children to drink water only, bestow on
them a fortune, the value and importance of which will be sensibly
felt through life.

MANY CHILDREN, HOWEVER, acquire a habit of drinking
during their meals; it would be more conducive to digestion, if they
were accustomed to drink only after having made a meal. This useful
rule is too often neglected, though it be certain that inundations of
the stomach, during the mastication and maceration of the food, not
only vitiate digestion, but they may be attended with other bad consequences; as cold drink, when brought in contact with the teeth
previously heated, may easily occasion cracks or chinks in these useful
bones, and pave the way for their carious dissolution.

IF WE INQUIRE INTO THE CAUSE, which produce the crying of
infants, we shall find that it seldom originates from pain, or
uncomfortable sensations; for those who are apt to imagine that such
causes must *always* operate on the body of an infant, are egregiously
mistaken; inasmuch as they conceive that the physical condition,
together with the method of expressing sensations, is the same in
infants and adults.

IT REQUIRES, however, no demonstration that the state of the
former is essentially different from that of the latter.

IN THE FIRST YEAR OF INFANCY, many expressions of the tender organs are to be considered only as efforts or manifestations of power.

WE OBSERVE, FOR INSTANCE, that a child, as soon as it is undressed or disencumbered from swaddling clothes, moves its arms and legs, and often makes a variety of strong exertions; yet no reasonable person would suppose that such attempts arise from a preternatural or oppressive state of the little agent.

IT IS THEREFORE EQUALLY ABSURD to drawn an unfavourable inference from every inarticulate cry; because, in most instances, these vociferating sounds imply the effort which children necessarily make to display the strength of their lungs, and exercise the organs of respiration.

NATURE has wisely ordained that by these very efforts the power and utility of functions so essential to life should be developed, and rendered more perfect with every inspiration.

HENCE it follows, that those over-anxious parents or nurses, who continually endeavour to prevent infants from crying, do them a material injury; for, by such imprudent management, their children seldom or never acquire a perfect form of the breast, while the foundation is laid in the pectoral vessels for obstructions, and other diseases.

INDEPENDENTLY of any particular causes, the cries of children, with regard to their general effects, are highly beneficial and necessary.

IN THE FIRST PERIOD OF LIFE, such exertions are the almost only exercise of the infant: thus the circulation of the blood, and all the other fluids, is rendered more uniform; digestion, nutrition, and the growth of the body, are thereby promoted; and the different secretions, together with the very important office of the skin, or insensible perspiration, are duly performed.

HENCE IT IS EXTREMELY IMPROPER to consider every noise of an infant as a claim upon our assistance, and to intrude either food or drink, with a view to satisfy its supposed wants. By such injudicious conduct, children readily acquire the injurious habit of demanding things, or nutriments, at improper times, and without necessity; their digestion becomes impaired; and consequently, at this early age, the whole mass of the fluids is gradually corrupted.

IF, HOWEVER, the mother or nurse has no recourse to the administration of aliment, they at least remove the child from its couch, carry it about, frequently in the middle of the night, and thus expose it to repeated colds, which are in their effects infinitely more dangerous than the most violent cries.

WE LEARN FROM DAILY EXPERIENCE, that children who have been the least indulged thrive much better, unfold all their faculties quicker, and acquire more muscular strength and vigour of mind than those who have been constantly favoured, and treated by their parents with the most solicitous attention: bodily weakness and mental imbecility are the usual attributes of the latter.

THE FIRST AND PRINCIPAL RULE OF EDUCATION ought never to be forgotten; that man is intended to be a free and independent agent; that his moral and physical powers ought to be *spontaneously* developed; and that he should as soon as possible be made acquainted with the nature and uses of all his faculties, in order to attain that degree of perfection which is consistent with the structure of his organs; and that he is not originally designed for what we endeavour to make of him by artificial aid.

HENCE THE GREATEST ART in educating children consists in the continual vigilance over all their actions, without ever giving them an opportunity of discovering that they are guided and watched.

THERE ARE, HOWEVER, instances in which the loud complaints of infants deserve our attention.

THUS, if their cries be unusually violent and long continued, we may conclude that they are troubled with colic pains; if, on such occasions, they move their arms and hands repeatedly towards the face, painful teething may account for the cause; and if other morbid phenomena accompany their cries, or if these expressions be repeated at certain periods of the day, we ought not to slight them, but endeavour to discover the proximate or remote causes.

INFANTS cannot sleep too long; and it is a favourable symptom, when they enjoy a calm and long-continued rest, of which they should by no means be deprived, as this is the greatest support granted to them by nature.

A CHILD LIVES, comparatively, much faster than an adult; its blood flows more rapidly; every stimulus operates more powerfully; and not only its constituent parts, but its vital resources also are more speedily consumed.

SLEEP PROMOTES A MORE CALM and uniform circulation of the blood; it facilitates the assimilation of the nutriment received, and contributes towards a more copious and regular deposition of alimentary matter, while the horizontal posture is the most favourable to the growth and development of the child.

SLEEP ought to be in proportion to the age of the infant. After the age of six months, the periods of sleep, as well as all other animal functions, may in some degree be regulated; yet, even then, a child should be suffered to sleep the whole night, and several hours both in the morning and in the afternoon.

MOTHERS AND NURSES SHOULD ENDEAVOUR to accustom infants, from the time of their birth, to sleep in the night preferably to the day, and for this purpose they ought to remove all external

impressions which may disturb their rest, such as noise, light, &c., but especially not to obey every call for taking them up, and giving food at improper times.

AFTER THE SECOND YEAR of their age, they will not instinctively require to sleep in the forenoon, though, after dinner it may be continued to the third and fourth year of life, if the child shows a particular inclination to repose; because, till that age, the full half of its time may safely be allotted to sleep.

FROM THAT PERIOD, however, it ought to be shortened for the space of one hour with every succeeding year; so that a child of seven years old may sleep about eight, and not exceeding nine hours: this proportion may be continued to the age of adolescence, and even manhood.

TO AWAKEN CHILDREN from their sleep with a noise, or in an impetuous manner, is extremely injudicious and hurtful: nor is it proper to carry them from a dark room immediately into a glaring light, or against a dazzling wall; for the sudden impression of light debilitates the organs of vision, and lays the foundation of weak eyes, from early infancy.

A BED-ROOM, or nursery, ought to be spacious and lofty, dry, airy, and not inhabited through the day.

NO SERVANTS, if possible should be suffered to sleep in the same room, and no linen or washed clothes should ever be hung there to dry, as they contaminate the air in which so considerable a portion of infantine life must be spent.

THE CONSEQUENCES attending a vitiated atmosphere in such rooms, are various, and often fatal.

FEATHER-BEDS should be banished from nurseries, as they are an unnatural and debilitating contrivance.

THE WINDOWS should never be opened at night, but left open the whole day, in fine clear weather.

LASTLY, THE BEDSTEAD must not be placed too low on the floor; nor is it proper to let children sleep on a couch which is made without any elevation from the ground; because the most mephitic and pernicious stratum of air in an apartment, is that within one or two feet from the floor, while the most wholesome, or atmospheric air, is in the middle of the room, and the inflammable gas ascends to the top.

FOOD FOR AN INFANT – Take of fresh cow's milk, one table-spoonful, and mix with two tablespoonfuls of hot water; sweeten with loaf-sugar as much as may be agreeable. This quantity is sufficient for once feeding a new-born infant; and the same quantity may be given every two or three hours, not oftener – till the mother's breast affords natural nourishment.

MILK FOR INFANTS SIX MONTHS OLD – Take one pint of milk, one pint of water; boil it, and add one tablespoonful of flour. Dissolve the flour first in half a teacupful of water; it must be strained in gradually, and boiled hard twenty minutes. As the child grows older, one third water. If properly made, it is the most nutritious, at the same time the most delicate food that can be given to young children.

BROTH – Made of lamb or chicken, with stale bread toasted, and broken in, is safe and healthy for the dinners of children, when first weaned.

MILK – Fresh from the cow, with a *very* little loaf-sugar, is good and safe food for young children. From three years old to seven, pure milk, into which is crumbled stale bread, is the best breakfast and supper for a child.

FOR A CHILD'S LUNCHEON – Good sweet butter, with stale bread, is one of the most nutritious, at the same time the most wholesome articles of food, that can be given children after they are weaned.

MILK PORRIDGE – Stir four tablespoonfuls of oatmeal, smoothly, into a quart of milk, then stir it quickly into a quart of boiling water, and boil up a few minutes till it is thickened: sweeten with sugar. Oatmeal, where it is found to agree with the stomach, is much better for children, being a fine opener as well as cleanser; fine flour in every shape is the reverse. Where biscuit-powder is in use, let it be made at home; this, at all events, will prevent them getting the sweepings of the baker's counters, boxes, and baskets. All the left bread in the nursery, hard ends of stale loaves, &c., ought to be dried in the oven or screen, and reduced to powder in the mortar.

MEATS FOR CHILDREN – Mutton, lamb, and poultry, are the best. Birds and the white meat of fowls, are the most delicate food of this kind that can be given. These meats should be slowly cooked, and no gravy, if made rich with butter, should be eaten by a young child. Never give children hard, tough, half-worked meats, of any kind.

VEGETABLES, EGGS, &C. FOR CHILDREN – Their rice ought to be cooked in no more water than is necessary to swell it; their apples roasted, or stewed with no more water than is necessary to steam them; their vegetables so well cooked as to make them require little butter, and less digestion; their eggs boiled slow and soft. The boiling of their milk ought to be directed by the state of their bowels; if flatulent or bilious, a very little curry-powder may be given in their vegetables with good effect – such as turmeric and the warm seeds (not hot peppers) are particularly useful in such cases.

POTATOES AND PEAS – Potatoes, particularly some kinds, are not easily digested by children; but this is easily remedied by mashing them very fine, and seasoning them with sugar and a little milk. When peas are dressed for children, let them be seasoned with mint and sugar, which will take off the flatulency. If they are old, let them be pulped, as the skins are perfectly indigestible by children's or weak stomachs. Never give them vegetables less stewed than would pulp through a colander.

RICE PUDDING WITH FRUIT – In a pint of new milk put two large spoonfuls of rice, well washed; then add two apples, pared and quartered, or a few currants or raisins. Simmer slowly till the rice is very soft, then add one egg, beaten, to bind it. Serve with cream and sugar.

PUDDINGS AND PANCAKES FOR CHILDREN – Sugar and egg, browned before the fire, or dropped as fritters into a hot frying-pan, without fat, will make them a nourishing meal.

TO PREPARE FRUIT FOR CHILDREN – A far more wholesome way than in pies or puddings, is to put apples sliced, or plums, currants, gooseberries, &c., into a stone jar; and sprinkle among them as much sugar as necessary. Set the jar in an oven on a hearth, with a teacupful of water to prevent the fruit from burning; or put the jar into a saucepan of water till its contents be perfectly done. Slices of bread, or some rice may be put into the jar, to eat with the fruit.

RICE AND APPLES – Core as many nice apples as will fill the dish; boil them in light syrup; prepare a quarter of a pound of rice in milk, with sugar and salt; put some of the rice in the dish, and put in the apples, and fill up the intervals with rice, and bake it in the oven till it is a fine colour.

A NICE APPLE CAKE FOR CHILDREN – Grate some stale bread, and slice about double the quantity of apples; butter a mould, and line it with sugar paste, and strew in some crumbs, mixed with a little sugar; then lay in apples, with a few bits of butter over them, and so continue till the dish is full; cover it with crumbs, or prepared rice; season with cinnamon and sugar. Bake it well.

FRUITS FOR CHILDREN – That fruits are naturally healthy in their season, if rightly taken, no one who believes that the Creator is a kind and beneficent Being can doubt. And yet the use of summer fruits appears often to cause most fatal diseases, especially in children. Why is this? Because we do not conform to the natural laws in using this kind of diet. These laws are very simple and easy to understand. Let the fruit be ripe when you eat it; and eat when you require *food*. Fruits that have *seeds* are much healthier than the *stone* fruits. But all fruits are better, for very young children, if baked or cooked in some manner, and eaten with bread. The French always eat bread with raw fruit. Apples and winter pears are very excellent food for children, indeed, for almost any person in health; but best when eaten for breakfast or dinner. If taken late in the evening, fruit often proves injurious. The old saying that apples are *gold in the morning, silver at noon, and lead at night*, is pretty near the truth. Both apples and pears are often good and nutritious when baked or stewed, for those delicate constitutions that cannot bear raw fruit. Much of the fruit gathered when unripe, might be rendered fit for food by preserving in sugar.

RIPE CURRANTS are excellent food for children. Mash the fruit, sprinkle with sugar, and with good bread let them eat of this fruit freely.

BLACKBERRY JAM – Gather the fruit in dry weather; allow half a pound of good brown sugar to every pound of fruit; boil the whole together gently for an hour, or till the blackberries are soft, stirring and mashing them well. Preserve it like any other jam, and it will be found very useful in families, particularly for children – regulating their bowels, and enabling you to dispense with cathartics. It may be spread on bread, or on puddings, instead of butter: and even when the blackberries are bought, it is cheaper than butter. In the country, every family should preserve, at least, half a peck of blackberries.

TO MAKE SENNA AND MANNA PALATABLE – Take half an ounce, when mixed, senna and manna; put in half a pint of boiling water; when the strength is abstracted, pour into the liquid from a quarter to half a pound of prunes and two large tablespoonfuls of W.I.

molasses. Stew slowly until the liquid is nearly absorbed. When cold it can be eaten with bread and butter, without detecting the senna, and is excellent for costive children.

DAUGHTERS – Mothers, who wish not only to discharge well their own duties in the domestic circle, but to train up their daughters at a later day to make happy and comfortable firesides for their families, should watch well, and guard well, the notions which they imbibe and with which they grow up. There will be so many persons ready to fill their young heads with false and vain fancies, and there is so much always afloat in society opposed to duty and common sense, that if mothers do not watch well, they may contract ideas very fatal to their future happiness and usefulness, and hold them till they grow into habits of thought or feeling. A wise mother will have her eyes open, and be ready for every case. A few words of common, downright, respectable, practical sense, timely uttered by her, may be enough to counteract some foolish idea or belief put into her daughter's head by others, whilst, if it be left unchecked, it may take such possession of the mind that it cannot later be corrected. One main falsity abroad in this age is the notion, that women, unless compelled to it by absolute poverty, are out of place when engaged in domestic affairs.

Now, mothers should have a care lest their daughters get hold of this conviction as regards themselves – there is danger of it; the fashion of the day endangers it, and the care that an affectionate family take to keep a girl, during the time of her education, free from other occupations than those of her tasks or her recreations, also endangers it. It is possible that affection may err in pushing this care too far; for as education means a fitting for life, and as a woman's life is much connected with domestic and family affairs, or ought to be so, if the indulgent consideration of parents abstains from all demands upon the young pupil of the school not connected with her books or her play, will she not naturally infer that the matters with which she is never asked to concern herself are, in fact, no concern to her, and that any attention she ever may bestow on them is not a matter of simple duty, but of grace, or concession, or stooping, on her part? Let mothers avoid such danger. If they would do so, they must bring up their daughters from the *first* with the idea that in this world it is required to give as well as to receive, to minister as well as to enjoy; that every person is bound to be useful, practically, literally useful, in his own sphere, and that a woman's first sphere is the house, and its concerns and demands. Once really imbued with this belief, and taught to see how much the comfort and happiness of woman herself, as well as of her family, depends on this part of her discharge of duty, and a young girl will usually be anxious to learn all that her mother is disposed to teach, and will be proud and happy to aid in any domestic occupations assigned to her, which need never be made so heavy as to interfere with the peculiar duties of her age, or its peculiar delights. If a mother wishes to see her daughter become a good, happy, and rational woman, never let her admit of contempt for domestic occupations, or even suffer them to be deemed secondary. They may be varied in character by station, but they can never be secondary to a woman.

HEALTH IN YOUTH – Late hours, irregular habits, and want of attention to diet, are common errors with most young men, and these gradually, but at first imperceptibly, undermine the health, and lay the foundation for various forms of disease in after life. It is a very difficult thing to make young persons comprehend this. They frequently sit up as late as twelve, one, or two o'clock, without experiencing any ill effects; they go without a meal to-day, and to-morrow eat to repletion, with only temporary inconvenience. One night they will sleep three or four hours, and the next nine or ten; or one night, in their eagerness to get away into some agreeable company, they will take no food at all; and the next, perhaps, will eat a hearty supper, and go to bed upon it. These, with various other irregularities, are common to the majority of young men, and are, as just stated, the cause of much bad health in mature life. Indeed, nearly all the shattered constitutions with which too many are cursed, are the result of a disregard to the plainest precepts of health in early life.

DOGS – The best way to keep a dog healthy is to let him have plenty of exercise, and not to over-feed him. Let them at all times have a plentiful supply of clean water, and encourage them to take to swimming, as it assists their cleanliness. When you wash them do not use a particle of soap, or you will prevent their licking themselves, and they may become habitually dirty. Properly treated, dogs should be fed only once a-day. Meat boiled for dogs, and the liquor in which it is boiled thickened with barley meal, or oatmeal, forms capital food. The distemper is liable to attack dogs from four months to four years old. It prevails most in spring and autumn. The disease is known by dullness of the eye, husky cough, shivering, loss of appetite and spirits, and fits. When fits occur, the dog will most likely die, unless a veterinary surgeon is called in. During the distemper, dogs should be allowed to run on the grass; their diet should be spare; and a little sulphur be placed in their water. Chemists who dispense cattle medicines can generally advise with sufficient safety upon the diseases of dogs, and it is best for unskilful persons to abstain from physicking them. Hydrophobia is the most dreadful of all diseases. The first symptoms are attended by thirst, fever, and languor. The dog starts convulsively in his sleep, and when awake, though restless, is languid. When a dog is suspected, he should be firmly chained in a place where neither children nor dogs or cats can get near him. Any one going to attend him should wear thick leather gloves, and proceed with great caution. When a dog snaps savagely at an imaginary object, it is almost a certain indication of madness; and when it exhibits a terror of fluids, it is confirmed hydrophobia. Some dogs exhibit a great dislike of musical sounds, and when this is the case they are too frequently made sport of. But it is a dangerous sport, as dogs have sometimes been driven mad by it. In many diseases dogs will be benefited by warm baths. The mange is a contagious disease, which it is difficult to get rid of when once contracted. The best way is to apply to a veterinary chemist for an ointment, and to keep applying it for some time after the disease has disappeared, or it will break out again.

CATS – It is generally supposed that cats are more attached to places than to individuals, but this is an error. They obstinately cling to certain places, because it is there they expect to see the persons to whom they are attached. A cat will return to an empty house, and remain in it for many weeks. But when at last she finds that the family does not return, she strays away, and if she chances then to find the family, she will abide with them. The same rules of feeding which apply to dogs apply also to cats. They should not be over-fed, nor too frequently. Cats are liable to the same diseases as dogs; though they do not become ill so frequently. A little brimstone in their milk occasionally is a good preventive. The veterinary chemist will also prescribe for the serious diseases of cats.

RABBITS should be kept dry and warm. Their best food is celery, parsley, and carrots; but they will eat almost any kind of vegetable, especially the dandelion, milk-thistle, &c. In spring it is recommended to give them tares. A little bran, and any kind of grain occasionally is beneficial, as too much green food is very hurtful. Care should be taken not to over-feed them. When fed upon dry food, a little skim milk will be a good drink for them. Tea-leaves, in small quantities, are said to be good for them.

GUINEA PIGS very much resemble rabbits in their living, and may be treated nearly the same. They should be kept dry, warm, and very clean.

WHITE MICE are fed upon bread soaked in milk; peas, oats, beans, &c., and any kind of nuts.

MONKEYS feed upon bread, and fruit of any kind. It is bad to give them meat, except, perhaps, small bones.

PARROTS may best be taught to talk by covering the cage at night, or rather in the evening, and then repeating to them slowly and distinctly the words they are desired to learn. They should be kept away from places where they would be liable to hear disagreeable noises, such as street cries, and the whistling and shouts of boys at play, or they will imitate them, and become too noisy to be peaceable. Parrots may be fed upon soaked bread, biscuit, mashed potatoes, and rape seed. They are fond of nuts. Cayenne pepper, sprinkled upon a bone, and given to them occasionally, is said to be very beneficial. They should be kept very clean, and allowed a bath frequently. It would be difficult to point out modes of treatment of the diseases of parrots. When they become affected in any way, it is best to keep them warm, change their food for a time, and give them lukewarm water to bathe in.

CANARIES – To distinguish a cock-bird from a hen, observe the bird when it is singing, and if it be a cock you will perceive the throat heaving with a pulse-like motion, a peculiarity which is scarcely perceptible in the hen.

Feed young canaries with white and yolk of hard egg, mixed together with a little bread steeped in water. This should be pressed and placed in one vessel, while in another should be put some boiled rape-seed, washed in fresh water. Change the food every day. When they are a month old, put them into separate cages.

Cut the claws of cage birds occasionally, when they become too long, but in doing so be careful not to draw blood.

BULLFINCHES – Old birds should be fed with German Paste, No. 2, and occasionally rape-seed. The Germans occasionally give them a little poppy-seed, and a grain or two of rice, steeped in Canary wine, when teaching them to pipe, as a reward for the progress they make.

Bird organs, or flageolets, are used to teach them. They breed three or four times a-year. The young require to be kept very warm, and to be fed every two hours with rape-seed, soaked for several hours in cold water, afterwards scalded and strained, bruised, mixed with bread, and moistened with milk. One, two, or three mouthfuls at a time.

SQUIRRELS – In a domestic state these little animals are fed with hazel nuts, or indeed any kind of nuts; and occasionally bread and milk. They should be kept very clean.

MISCHIEF-MAKERS

Oh! could there in this world be found
Some little spot of happy ground,
Where village pleasures might go round
Without the village tattling!
How doubly blest that place would be,
Where all might dwell in liberty,
Free from the bitter misery
Of gossips' endless prattling.

If such a spot were really known,
Dame Peace might claim it as her own;
And in it she might fix her throne,
For ever and for ever:
There, like a queen, might reign and live,
While every one would soon forgive
The little slights they might receive,
And be offended never.

'Tis mischief-makers that remove
Far from our hearts the warmth of love,
And lead us all to disapprove
What gives another pleasure,
They seem to take one's part – but when
They've heard our cares, unkindly then
They soon retail them all again,
Mix'd with their poisonous measure.

And then they've such a sunning way,
Of telling ill-meant tales: they say,
"Don't mention what I've said, I pray,
I would not tell another;"
Straight to your neighbour's house they go,
Narrating everything they know;

And break the peace of high and low,
Wife, husband, friend, and brother.

Oh! that the mischief-making crew
Were all reduced to one or two,
And they were painted red or blue,
That every one might know them
Then would our villagers forget
To rage and quarrel, fume and fret,
And fall into an angry pet,
With things so much below them.

For 'tis a sad, degrading part
To make another's bosom smart,
And plant a dagger in the heart
We ought to love and cherish
Then let us evermore be found
In quietness with all around,
While friendship, joy, and peace abound,
And angry feelings perish!

Household Management

DOMESTIC RULES – Mrs. Hamilton, in her "Cottagers of Glenburnie", gives three simple rules for the regulation of domestic affairs, which deserve to be remembered, and which would, if carried into practice, be the means of saving time, labour, and patience, and of making every house a "well ordered" one. They are as follows: – 1. Do everything in its proper time. 2. Keep everything to its proper use. 3. Put everything in its proper place.

TAKING A HOUSE – Before taking a house, be careful to calculate that the rent is not too high in proportion to your means; for remember that the rent is a claim that must be paid with but little delay, and that the landlord has greater power over your property than any other creditor.

HAVING DETERMINED the amount of rent which you can afford to pay, be careful to select the best house which can be obtained for that sum. And in making that selection let the following matters be carefully considered:–

FIRST – Carefully regard the healthfulness of the situation. Avoid the neighbourhood of graveyards, and of factories giving forth unhealthy vapours; avoid low and damp districts, the course of canals, and localities of reservoirs of water, gas works, &c.; make inquiries as to the drainage of the neighbourhood, and inspect the drainage and water supply of the premises. A house standing on an incline is likely to be better drained than one standing upon the summit of a hill, or on a level below a hill. Endeavour to obtain a position where the direct sunlight falls upon the house, for this is absolutely essential to health; and give preference to a house the openings of which are sheltered from the north and east winds.

SECOND – Consider the distance of the house from your place of occupation: and also its relation to provision markets, and the prices that prevail in the neighbourhood.

HAVING CONSIDERED THESE material and leading features, examine the house in detail, carefully looking into its state of repair; notice the windows that are broken; whether the chimneys smoke; whether the paper on the walls is damaged, especially in the lower parts, and the corners, by the skirtings; whether the locks, bolts, handles of doors, and window-fastenings are in proper condition; make a list of the fixtures; ascertain whether all rent and taxes were paid up by the previous tenant, and whether the party from whom you take the house is the original landlord, or his agent or tenant. And do not commit yourself by the signing of any agreement until you are satisfied upon all these points, *and see that all has been done which the landlord had undertaken.*

IF YOU ARE ABOUT TO FURNISH A HOUSE, do not spend all your money, be it much or little. Do not let the beauty of this thing, and the cheapness of that, tempt you to buy unnecessary articles. Doctor Franklin's maxim was a wise one – "Nothing is cheap that we do not want." Buy merely enough to get along with at first. It is only by experience that you can tell what will be the wants of your family. If you spend all your money, you will find you have purchased many things you do not want, and have no means left to get many things which you do want. If you have enough, and more than enough, to get everything suitable to your situation, do not think you must spend it all, merely because you happen to have it. Begin humbly. As riches increase, it is easy and pleasant to increase in comforts; but it is always painful and inconvenient to decrease. After all, these things are viewed in their proper light by the truly judicious and respectable. Neatness, tastefulness, and good sense may be shown in the management of a small household, and the arrangement of a little furniture, as well as upon a larger scale; and these qualities are always praised, and always treated with respect and attention. The consideration which many purchase by living beyond their income, and, of course, living upon others, is not worth the trouble it costs. The glare there is about this false and wicked parade is deceptive; it does not, in fact, procure a man valuable friends, or extensive influence.

HINTS FOR HOME COMFORTS

A short needle makes the most expedition in plain sewing.

When you are particular in wishing to have precisely what you want from a butcher's, go and purchase it yourself.

One flannel petticoat will wear nearly as long as two, if turned behind part before, when the front begins to wear thin.

People in general are not aware how very essential to the health of their inmates is the free admission of light into their houses.

A leather strap, with a buckle to fasten, is much more commodious than a cord for a box in general use for short distances; cording and uncording is a nasty job.

There is not any real economy in purchasing cheap calico for gentlemen's night shirts. The calico cuts in holes, and soon becomes bad coloured in washing.

Sitting to sew by candle-light by a table with a dark cloth on it is injurious to the eye-sight. When no other remedy presents itself, put a sheet of white paper before you.

People very commonly complain of indigestion: how can it be wondered at, when they seem by their habit of swallowing their food wholesale, to forget for what purpose they are provided with teeth.

Never allow your servants to put wiped knives on your table, for, generally speaking, you may see that they have been wiped with a dirty cloth. If a knife is brightly cleaned, they are compelled to use a clean cloth.

There is not anything gained in economy by having very young and inexperienced servants at low wages; they break, waste, and destroy more than an equivalent for higher wages, setting aside comfort and respectability.

No article in dress tarnishes so readily as black crape trimmings, and few things injure it more than damp: therefore, to preserve its beauty on bonnets, a lady in nice mourning should in her evening walks, at all seasons of the year, take as a companion an old parasol to shade her crape.

A piece of oil-cloth (about twenty inches long) is a useful appendage to a common sitting-room. Kept in the closet, it can be available at any time to place jars upon, &c. &c., which are likely to soil your table during the process of dispensing their contents: a wing and duster are harmonious accompaniments to the oil-cloth.

In most families many members are not fond of fat: servants seldom like it – consequently there is frequently much wasted; to avoid which, take off bits of suet fat from beefsteaks, &c., previous to cooking; they can be used for puddings. With good management there need not be any waste in any shape or form.

Nothing looks worse than shabby gloves; and, as they are expensive articles in dress, they require a little management. A good glove will last six cheap ones with care. Do not wear your best gloves to night church – the heat of the gas, &c., gives a moisture to the hands, that spoils the gloves; do not wear them in very wet weather; as carrying umbrellas, and drops of rain, spoil them.

A given quantity of tea is similar to malt – only giving strength to a given quantity of water, as we find therefore any additional quantity is waste. Two small teaspoonfuls of good black tea, and one three parts full of green, is sufficient to make three teacupfuls agreeable, the water being put in, in a boiling state at once: a second edition of water gives a vapid flavour to tea.

It may sound like being over particular, but we recommend persons to make a practice of fully addressing notes, &c., on all occasions; when, in case of their being dropped by careless messengers (which is not a rare occurrence), it is evident for whom they are intended, without undergoing the inspection of any other parties bearing a similar name.

Children should not be allowed to ask for the same thing twice. This may be accomplished by parents, teacher, (or whoever may happen to have the management of them), paying attention to their little wants, if proper, at once, when possible. The children should be instructed to understand that when they are not answered immediately, it is because it is not convenient. Let them learn patience by waiting.

We know not of anything attended with more serious consequences than that of sleeping in damp linen. Persons are frequently assured that they have been at a fire for many hours, but the question is as to what sort of fire, and whether they have been properly turned, so that every part may be exposed to the fire. The fear of creasing the linen, we know, prevents many from unfolding it, so as to be what we consider sufficiently aired; but health is of more importance than appearances: with gentleness there need be no fear of want of neatness.

If the weather appears doubtful, always take the precaution of having an umbrella when you go out, particularly in going to church; your thereby avoid incurring one of three disagreeables: in the first place, the chance of getting wet – or encroaching under a friend's umbrella – or being under the necessity of borrowing one, consequently involving the trouble of returning it, and possibly (as is the case nine times out of ten) inconveniencing your friend by neglecting to return it. Those who disdain the use of umbrellas generally appear with shabby hats, tumbled bonnet ribbons, wrinkled silk dresses, &c. &c., the consequence of frequent exposure to unexpected showers, to say nothing of colds taken, no one can tell how.

Exercise in the open air is of the first importance to the human frame, yet how many are in a manner deprived of it by their own want of management of their time! Females with slender means are for the most part destined to in-door occupations, and have but little time allotted them for taking the air, and that little time is generally sadly encroached upon by the ceremony of dressing to go out. It may appear a simple suggestion, but experience only will show how much time might be redeemed by

habits of regularity; such as putting the shawls, cloaks, gloves, shoes, clogs, &c., &c., or whatever is intended to be worn, in readiness, instead of having to search one drawer, then another, for possibly a glove or collar – wait for shoes being cleaned, &c., – and this when (probably) the out-going persons have to return to their employment at a given time. Whereas, if all were in readiness, the preparations might be accomplished in a few minutes, the walk not being curtailed by unnecessary delays.

Eat slowly and you will not over-eat.

Keeping the feet warm will prevent headaches.

Late at breakfast – hurried for dinner – cross at tea.

Between husband and wife little attentions beget much love.

Always lay your table neatly, whether you have company or not.

Put your balls or reels of cotton into little bags, leaving the ends out.

Whatever you may choose to give away, always be sure to *keep your temper*.

Dirty windows speak to the passer-by of the negligence of the inmates.

In cold weather, a leg of mutton improves by being hung three, four, or five weeks.

When meat is hanging, change its position frequently, to equally distribute the juices.

There is much more injury done by admitting visitors to invalids than is generally supposed.

Matches, out of the reach of children, should be kept in every bedroom. They are cheap enough.

Apple and suet dumplings are lighter when boiled in a net than a cloth. Scum the pot well.

When chamber towels get thin in the middle, cut them in two, sew the selvages together, and hem the sides.

HOW TO TAKE CARE OF YOUR HAT – If your hat is wet, shake it out as much as possible; then brush it with a soft brush as smooth as you can, or with a clean linen cloth or handkerchief; wipe it very carefully, keep the beaver flat and smooth, in the same direction as it was first placed; then, with a small cane, beat the nap gently up, and hang it up to dry in a cool place. When it is dry, lay it on a table, and brush it round several times with a soft brush in the proper direction; and you will find your hat not the least injured by the rain. If the gloss is not quite so high as you wish, take a flat iron, moderately heated, and pass the same two or three times gently over the hat; brush it afterwards, and it will become nearly as handsome as when sent home from the maker. – *To Scour a Hat when the*  *Nap is Clotted, and to take Salt Water out* – Get a hard brush, a basin of hot water (boiling), and some yellow soap; rub a little of the soap lightly on the brush and dip it into the water; brush the hat round with the nap. If you find the nap clotted, do not scrape it with your fingers, as that tears it off, but brush it until it is smooth, and the soap is thoroughly out; then take a piece of wood, or the back of a knife, and scrape it well round; you will find all the dirt come out; then beat it gently with a cane.

CARE OF LINEN – When linen is well dried and laid by for use, nothing more is necessary than to secure it from damp and insects; the latter may be agreeably performed by a judicious mixture of aromatic shrubs and flowers, cut up and sewed up in silken bags, to be interspersed among the drawers and shelves. These ingredients may consist of lavender, thyme, roses, cedar-shavings, powdered sassafras, cassia lignea, &c., into which a few drops of otto of roses, or other strong-scented perfume, may be thrown. In all cases, it will be found more consistent with economy to examine and repair all washable articles, more especially linen, that may stand in need of it, previous to sending them to the laundry. It will also be prudent to have every article carefully numbered, and so arranged, after washing, as to have their regular turn and term in domestic use.

HAIR DYE – A friend of ours, to whom we applied upon the subject, favoured us with the following information: – I have operated upon my own cranium for at least a dozen years, and though I have heard it affirmed that dying the hair will produce insanity, I am happy to think I am, as yet, perfectly sane, and under no fear of being otherwise; at all events, I am wiser than I once was, when I paid five

All the Fair,
With Beaming Eye and Curly Hair,
SING IN PRAISE OF THE
ACME
HAIR DYE.
*It will curl straight hair, and
straighten curled hair.*

shillings for what I can now make myself for less than twopence! – but to the question: – I procure lime, which I speedily reduce to powder by throwing a little water upon it, then mix this with litharge (three quarters lime, and a quarter litharge), which I sift through a fine hair sieve, and then I have what is sold at a high price under the name of "Unique Powder," and the most effectual hair dye that has yet been discovered. But the application of it is not very agreeable, though simple enough: – Put a quantity of it in a saucer, pour boiling water upon it, and mix it up with a knife like thick mustard; divide the hair into thin layers, with a comb, and plaster the mixture thickly into the layers to the roots, and all over the hair. When it is all completely covered over with it, then lay all over it a covering of damp blue, or brown paper, then bind over it, closely, a handkerchief, then put on a nightcap over all, and go to bed; in the morning, brush out the powder, wash thoroughly with soap and warm water, then dry, curl, oil, &c. I warrant that hair thus managed will be a permanent and beautiful black, which, I dare say, most people would prefer to either grey or red. Now, notwithstanding the patient endurance and satisfactory experience of our friend, we very much doubt, whether one person in a hundred, would be content to envelope their heads in batter of this description, and then retire to rest. To rest! did we say? We envy not the slumbers enjoyed under these circumstances. We fancy we can do something still better for those who are ashamed of their grey hairs. The hair dyes formerly used produced very objectionable tints. Latterly several perfumers have been selling dyes, consisting of two liquids to be used in succession, at exceedingly high prices, such as 7s., 14s., and 21s., a case. The composition has been kept a close secret in the hands of a few. The procuring of it for publication in this work has been attended with considerable difficulty, but our readers may take it as an earnest that no pains or expense will be spared to render really useful information.

BUG POISON – Proof spirit, one pint; camphor, two ounces; oil of turpentine, four ounces; corrosive sublimate, one ounce. Mix. Cost: proof spirit, 1s. 10d. per pint; camphor, 2s. 8d. per pound; oil of turpentine, 8d. per pint; corrosive sublimate, 3s. 6d. per pound.

GLORIOUS INTELLIGENCE!
ANOTHER DREADFUL SORTIE REPULSED!
LORD DUNDONALD OUTDONE!

THE ABOVE were the exclamations with which a gentleman rushed into the office of "ENQUIRE WITHIN" a few days ago. "What's the matter?" we asked; "any news from the Crimea?" "The Crimea! No. But you just put this piece of information in your work, and thousands will thank you for it. We have been for a long time troubled with bugs, and never could get rid of them by any clean, inoffensive, and expeditious method, until a friend of ours told us to suspend a small bag of camphor to the bed, just in the centre, overhead. We did so, and the enemy was most effectually repulsed, and has not made his appearance since – not even for a reconnaissance!" We therefore give the information upon this method of getting rid of bugs, our informant being most confident of its success in every case.

HONEY SOAP – Cut thin two pounds of yellow soap into a double saucepan, occasionally stirring it till it is melted, which will be in a few minutes if the water is kept boiling around it; then add a quarter of a pound of palm oil, quarter of a pound of honey, three pennyworth of true oil of cinnamon; let all boil together another six or eight minutes; pour out and stand it by till next day, it is then fit for immediate use. If made as these directions it will be found to be a very superior soap.

TO DISTINGUISH MUSHROOMS FROM POISONOUS FUNGI:– 1. Sprinkle a little salt on the spongy part or gills of the sample to be tried. If they turn yellow, they are poisonous, if black, they are wholesome. Allow the salt to act before you decide on the question. – 2. False mushrooms have a warty cap, or else fragments of membrane, adhering to the upper surface, are heavy, and emerge from a vulva or bag; they grow in tufts or clusters in woods, on the stumps of trees, &c., whereas the true mushrooms grow in pastures. – 3. False mushrooms have an astringent, styptic, and disagreeable taste. – 4. When cut they turn blue. – 5. They are moist on the surface and generally. – 6. Of a rose or orange colour. – 7. The gills of the true mushroom are of a pinky red, changing to a liver colour. – 8. The flesh is white. – 9. The stem is white, solid, and cylindrical.

LAVENDER SCENT BAG – Take of lavender flowers free from stalk half a pound; dried thyme and mint of each half an ounce; ground cloves and caraways of each a quarter of an ounce; common slat, dried, one ounce; mix the whole well together, and put the product into silk or cambric bags. In this way it will perfume the drawers and linen very nicely.

TO RENOVATE SILKS – Sponge faded silks with warm water and soap, then rub them with a dry cloth on a flat board; afterwards iron them on the *inside* with a smoothing iron. Old black silks may be improved by sponging with spirits; in this case, the ironing may be done on the right side, thin paper being spread over to prevent glazing.

SUBSTITUTE FOR CREAM IN TEA OR COFFEE – Beat the white of an egg to a froth, put to it a very small lump of butter, and mix well. Then turn into it gradually, so that it may not curdle. If perfectly done, it will be an excellent substitute for cream.

STAINS AND MARKS FROM BOOKS – A solution of oxalic acid, citric acid, or tartaric acid, is attended with the least risk, and may be

applied upon the paper and prints without fear of damage. These acids, taking out writing ink, and not touching the printing, can be used for restoring books where the margins have been written upon, without attacking the text.

TO EXTRACT GREASE SPOTS FROM BOOKS OR PAPER –
Gently warm the greased or spotted part of the book or paper, and
then press upon it pieces of blotting-paper, one after another, so as to
absorb as much of the grease as possible. Have ready some fine clear
essential oil of turpentine heated almost to a boiling state, warm the
greased leaf a little, and then, with a soft clean brush, wet the heated
turpentine both sides of the spotted part. By repeating this
application, the grease will be extracted. Lastly, with another brush,
dipped in rectified spirits of wine, go over the place, and the grease
will no longer appear, neither will the paper be discoloured.

TO PRESERVE MILK – Provide bottles, which must be perfectly
clean, sweet, and dry; draw the milk from the cow into the bottles,
and as they are filled, immediately cork with pack-thread or wire.
Then spread a little straw at the bottom of a boiler, on which place
bottles with straw between them, until the boiler contains a sufficient
quantity. Fill it up with cold water; heat the water, and as soon as it
begins to boil, draw the fire, and let the whole gradually cool. When
quite cold, take out the bottles and pack them in saw-dust, in hampers,
and stow them in the coolest part of the house. Milk preserved in this
manner, and allowed to remain even eighteen months in the bottles,
will be as sweet as when first milked from the cow.

TO LOOSEN GLASS STOPPERS OF BOTTLES – With a feather
rub a drop or two of salad oil round the stopper, close to the mouth of
the bottle or decanter, which must be then placed before the fire, at the
distance of about eighteen inches; the heat will cause the oil to
insinuate itself between the stopper and the neck. When the bottle or
decanter has grown warm, gently strike the stopper on one side, and
then on the other, with any light wooden instrument; then try it with
the hand: if it will not yet move, place it again before the fire, adding
another drop of oil. After a while strike again as before, and, by
persevering in this process, however tightly it may be fastened in, you
will at length succeed in loosening it.

HOW TO REMOVE STAINS FROM FLOORS – For removing spots of grease from boards, take equal parts of fullers' earth and pearlash, a quarter of a pound of each, and boil in a quart of soft water; and, while hot, lay it on the greased parts, allowing it to remain on them for ten or twelve hours; after which it may be scoured off with sand and water. A floor much spotted with grease should be completely washed over with this mixture the day before it is scoured. Fullers' earth or ox-gall, boiled together, form a very powerful cleansing mixture for floors or carpets. Stains of ink are removed by strong vinegar, or salts of lemon will remove them.

CARPETS – If the corner of a carpet gets loose and prevents the door opening, or trips every one up that enters the room, nail it down at once. A dog's-eared carpet marks the sloven as well as the dog's-eared book. An English gentleman, travelling some years ago in Ireland, took a hammer and tacks with him, because he found dog's-eared carpets at all the inns where he rested. At one of these inns he tacked down the carpet which, as usual, was loose near the door, and soon afterwards rang for his dinner. While the carpet was loose the door could not be opened without a hard push; so when the waiter came up, he just unlatched the door, and then going back a couple of yards, he rushed against it, as his habit was, with a sudden spring to force it open. But the wrinkles of the carpet were no longer there to stop it, and not meeting with the expected resistance, the unfortunate waiter fell full sprawl into the room. It had never entered his head that so much trouble might be saved by means of a hammer and half-a-dozen tacks, until his fall taught him that make-shift is a very unprofitable kind of shift. There are a good many houses in England where a similar practical lesson might be of service.

OINTMENT FOR SCURF IN THE HEADS OF INFANTS – Lard, two ounces; sulphuric acid, diluted, two drachms; rub them together, and anoint the head once a day.

RANCID BUTTER – This may be restored by melting it in a water bath, with some coarsely powdered animal charcoal (which has been thoroughly sifted from dust), and strained through flannel.

REMEDY FOR BLISTERED FEET FROM LONG WALKING – Rub the feet, at going to bed, with spirits mixed with tallow dropped from a lighted candle into the palm of the hand.

CURE FOR CHAPPED HANDS – Instead of washing the hands with soap employ oatmeal, and after each washing take a little dry oatmeal, and rub over the hands, so as to absorb any moisture.

DR. BIRT DAVIES' GOUT MIXTURE – Wine of colchicum, one ounce; spirit of nitrous ether, one ounce; iodine of potassium, two scruples; distilled water, two ounces. Mix. A teaspoonful in camomile tea two or three times a day.

TO RENDER LINEN, &C., INCOMBUSTIBLE – All linen, cotton, muslins, &c., when dipped in a solution of the pure vegetable alkali at a gravity of from 124 to 130 (taking water at the gravity of 100) become incombustible.

DR. BABINGTON'S MIXTURE FOR INDIGESTION – Infusion of calumba, six ounces; carbonate of potassa, one drachm; compound tincture of gentian, three drachms. Mix. Dose, two or three tablespoonfuls daily at noon.

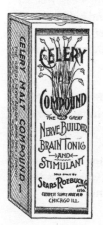

TO TAKE STAINS OF WINE OUT OF LINEN – Hold the articles in milk that is boiling on the fire, and the stains will soon disappear.

DR. CLARK'S PILLS FOR NERVOUS HEAD-ACHE – Socotrine aloes, powdered rhubarb, of each one drachm; compound powder of cinnamon, one scruple; hard soap, half a drachm; syrup enough to form the mass. To be divided into fifty pills, of which two will be sufficient for a dose; to be taken occasionally.

AN EFFECTUAL LIME FOR THE DESTRUCTION OF BUGS – Two ounces of red arsenic, a quarter of a pound of white soap, half an ounce of camphor dissolved in a teaspoonful of spirits rectified, made into a paste of the consistency of cream: place this mixture in the openings and cracks of the bedstead.

MIXTURE FOR DESTROYING FLIES – Infusion of quassia, one pint; brown sugar, four ounces; ground pepper, two ounces. To be well mixed together and put in small shallow dishes when required.

ERASMUS WILSON'S LOTION TO PROMOTE THE GROWTH OF THE HAIR – Eau de Cologne, two ounces; tincture of cantharides, two drachms; oil of rosemary and oil of lavender; of each, ten drops.

DR. SCOTT'S WASH TO WHITEN THE NAILS – Diluted sulphuric acid, two drachms; tincture of myrrh, one drachm; spring water, four ounces. Mix. First cleanse with white soap, and then dip the fingers into the wash.

CURE FOR CORNS – Take two ounces of gum ammoniac, two ounces of yellow wax and six drachms of verdigris, melt them together, and spread the composition on soft leather. Cut away as much of the corn as you can, then apply the plaster, and renew it every fortnight till the corn is away.

DEAFNESS FROM DEFICIENT SECRETION OF WAX – Take oil of turpentine, half a drachm; olive oil, two drachms. Mix. Two drops to be introduced into the ear at bed-time.

IMPRESSIONS FROM COINS – Melt a little isinglass glue with brandy, and pour it thinly over the medal, &c., so as to cover its whole surface; let it remain on for a day or two, till it has thoroughly dried and hardened, and then take it off, when it will be fine, clear, and as hard as a piece of Muscovy glass, and will have a very elegant impression of the coin. It will also resist the effects of damp air, which occasions all other kinds of glue to soften and bend if not prepared in this way.

TRAP FOR SNAILS – Snails are particularly fond of bran; if a little is spread on the ground, and covered over with a few cabbage-leaves or tiles, they will congregate under them in great numbers, and by examining them every morning, and destroying them, their numbers will be materially decreased.

TO DESTROY SLUGS – Slugs are very voracious, and their ravages often do considerable damage, not only to the kitchen garden, but to the flower-beds also. If, now and then, a few slices of turnip be put about the beds, on a summer or autumnal evening, the slugs will congregate thereon, and may be destroyed.

TO KEEP MOTHS, BEETLES, &C., FROM THE CLOTHES – Put a piece of camphor in a linen bag, or some aromatic herbs, in the drawers, among linen or woollen clothes, and neither moth nor worm will come near them.

TO CLEAR ROSE TREES FROM BLIGHT – Take sulphur and tobacco dust in equal quantities, and strew it over the trees of a morning when the dew is on them. The insects will disappear in a few days. The trees should then be syringed with a decoction of elder leaves.

TO PREVENT MILDEW ON ALL SORTS OF TREES – The best preventive against mildew is to keep the plant subject to it occasionally syringed with a decoction of elder leaves, which will prevent the fungus growing on them.

OFFENSIVE BREATH – For this purpose, almost the only substance that should be admitted at the toilette is the concentrated

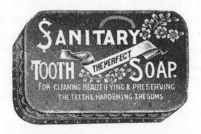

solution of chloride of soda. From six or ten drops of it in a wine glass full of pure spring water, taken immediately after the operations of the morning are completed.

TO DETECT COPPER IN PICKLES OR GREEN TEA – Put a few leaves of the tea, or some of the pickle, cut small, into a phial with two or three drachms of liquid ammonia, diluted with one half the quantity of water. Shake the phial, when, if the most minute portion of copper be present, the liquid will assume a fine blue colour.

IN SOME CASES, the odour arising from carious teeth is combined with that of the stomach. If the mouth be well rinsed with a teaspoonful of the solution of the chloride in a tumbler of water, the bad odour of the teeth will be removed.

TO PROTECT DAHLIAS FROM EARWIGS – Dip a piece of wool or cotton in oil, and slightly tie it round the stalk, about a foot from the earth. The stakes which you will put into the ground to support your plants must also be surrounded by the oiled cotton or wool, or the insects will climb up them to the blossoms and tender tops of the stems.

TO FREE PLANTS FROM LEAF-LICE – M. Braun, of Vienna, gives the following as a cheap and easy mode of effecting it: – Mix one ounce of flowers of sulphur with one bushel of sawdust; scatter this over the plants infected with these insects, and they will soon be freed, though a second application may possibly be necessary.

TREATMENT OF WARTS – Pare the hard and dried skin from their tops, and then touch them with the smallest drop of strong acetic acid, taking care that the acid does not run off the wart upon the neighbouring skin, for if it do, it will occasion inflammation and much pain. If this practice be continued once or twice daily, *with regularity*, paring the surface of the wart occasionally, when it gets hard and dry, the wart may be soon effectually cured.

TO EXTERMINATE BEETLES – 1. Place a few lumps of unslaked lime where they frequent. 2. Set a dish or trap containing a little beer or syrup at the bottom, and place a few sticks slanting against its sides, so as to form a sort of gangway for the beetles to climb up by, when they will go headlong into the bait set for them. 3. Mix equal weights of red lead, sugar, and flour, and place it nightly near their haunts. This mixture made into sheets, forms the beetle wafers sold at the oil shops.

TO CLEAN HAIR BRUSHES – As hot water and soap very soon soften the hairs, and rubbing completes their destruction, use soda, dissolved in cold water, instead; soda having an affinity for grease, it cleans the brush with little friction. Do not set them near the fire, nor in the sun, to dry, but after shaking them well, set them on the point of the handle in a shady place.

TO CLEAN FRENCH KID GLOVES – Put the gloves on your hand and wash them, as if you were washing your hands, in some spirits of turpentine, until quite clean; then hang them up in a warm place, or where there is a current of air, and all smell of the turpentine will be removed. This method is practised in Paris, and since its introduction into this country, thousands of pounds have been gained by it.

EASY METHOD OF BREAKING GLASS TO ANY REQUIRED FIGURE – Make a small notch by means of a file on the edge of a piece of glass, then make the end of a tobacco-pipe, or of a rod of iron of the same size, red hot in the fire, apply the hot iron to the notch, and draw it slowly along the surface of the glass in any direction you please, a crack will follow the direction of the iron.

GLASS should be washed in cold water, which gives it a brighter and clearer look than when cleansed with warm water.

READING IN BED at night should be avoided, as, besides the danger of an accident, it never fails to injure the eyes.

FLOWERS and shrubs should be excluded from a bed-chamber.

WATER of every kind, except rain water, will speedily cover the inside of a tea-kettle with an unpleasant crust; this may easily be guarded against by placing a clean oyster-shell in the tea-kettle, which will always keep in good order, by attracting the particles of earth or of stone.

IN MAKING COFFEE, observe that the broader the bottom and the smaller the top of the vessel, the better it will be.

THE WHITE OF AN EGG well beaten with quicklime, and a small quantity of very old cheese, forms an excellent substitute for cement, when wanted in a hurry, either for broken china or old ornamental glass ware.

EGGS MAY BE PRESERVED by applying with a brush a solution of gum-arabic to the shells, and afterwards packing them in dry charcoal dust.

TO RENDER SHOES WATERPROOF – Warm a little bee's-wax and mutton suet until it is liquid, and rub some of it slightly over the edges of the sole where the stitches are.

MOUTH GLUE – A very useful preparation is sold by many of the law stationers in London under this title; it is merely a thin cake of soluble glue (four inches by one and a half), which, when moistened with the tongue, furnishes a ready means of fastening papers, &c., together. It is made by dissolving one pound of fine glue or gelatine in water, and adding half a pound of brown sugar, boiling the whole until it is sufficiently thick to become solid on cooling; it is then poured into moulds or on a slab slightly greased, and cut into the required shape when cool. Cost: gelatine 1s. 3d. per pound; sugar, 4d. per pound.

FAMILY TOOL CHESTS – Much inconvenience, and considerable expense might be saved, if it was the general custom to keep in every house certain tools for the purpose of performing at home what are

called small jobs, instead of being always obliged to send for a mechanic and pay him for executing little things that, in most cases, could be sufficiently well done by a man or boy belonging to the family, provided that the proper instruments were at hand.

THE COST of these articles is very trifling, and the advantages of having them always in the house are far beyond the expense.

FOR INSTANCE, there should be an axe, a hatchet, a saw (a large woodsaw also, with a buck or stand, if wood is burned), a claw-hammer, a mallet, two gimlets of different sizes, two screwdrivers, a chisel, a small plane, one or two jack-knives, a pair of large scissors or shears, and a carpet fork or stretcher.

ALSO AN ASSORTMENT OF NAILS of various sizes, from large spikes down to small tacks, not forgetting brass-headed nails, some larger and some smaller.

SCREWS, likewise, will be found very convenient, and hooks on which to hang things.

THE NAILS AND SCREWS should be kept in a wooden box, made with divisions to separate the various sorts, for it is very troublesome to have them mixed.

AND LET CARE BE TAKEN to keep up the supply, lest it should run out unexpectedly, and the deficiency cause delay and incon-venience at a time when their use is wanted.

IT IS WELL to have somewhere, in the lower part of the house, a deep light closet, appropriated entirely to tools and things of equal utility, for executing promptly such little repairs as convenience may require, without the delay or expense of procuring an artisan. This closet should have at least one large shelf, and that about three feet from the floor.

BENEATH this shelf may be a deep drawer, divided into two compartments. This drawer may contain cakes of glue, pieces of chalk, and balls of twine of different size and quality.

THERE may be shelves at the sides of the closet for glue-pots, paste-pots, and brushes, pots for black, white, green, and red paint, cans of painting oils, paint-brushes, &c.

AGAINST the wall, above the large shelf, let the tools be suspended, or laid across nails or hooks of proper size to support them.

THIS is much better than keeping them in a box, where they may be injured by rubbing against each other, and the hand may be hurt in feeling among them to find the thing that is wanted.

BUT when hung up against the back wall of the closet, of course each tool can be seen at a glance.

WE have been shown an excellent and simple contrivance for designating the exact places allotted to all these articles in a very complete tool closet.

ON THE CLOSET WALL, directly under the large nails that support the tools, is drawn with a small brush dipped in black paint or ink, an outline representation of the tool or instrument belonging to that particular place.

FOR INSTANCE, under each saw is sketched the outline of that saw, under each gimlet a sketch of that gimlet, under the screw-drivers are slight drawings of screw-drivers.

SO THAT WHEN bringing back any tool that has been taken away for use, the exact spot to which it belongs can be found in a moment; and all confusion in putting them up and finding them again is thus prevented.

A HINT ON HOUSEHOLD MANAGEMENT – Have you ever observed what a dislike servants have to anything cheap. They hate saving their master's money. I tried this experiment with great success the other day. Finding we consumed a vast deal of soap, I sat down in my thinking chair, and took the soap question into consideration, and I found reason to suspect we were using a very expensive article, where a much cheaper one would serve the purpose better. I ordered half a dozen pounds of both sorts, but took the precaution of changing the papers on which the prices were marked before giving them into the hands of Betty. "Well, Betty, which soap do you find washes best?" "Oh, please sir, the dearest, in the blue paper; it makes a lather as well again as the other." "Well, Betty, you shall always have it then;" and thus the unsuspecting Betty saved me some pounds a year, and washed the clothes better. – *Rev. Sidney Smith.*

SERVANTS – There are frequent complaints that, in these days, servants are bad, and apprentices are bad, and dependants and aiding hands generally are bad. It may be so. But if it is so, what is the inference? In the working of the machine of society, class moves pretty much with class; that is, one class moves pretty much with its equals in the community (equals so far as social station is concerned), and apart from other classes, as much those below as those above itself; but there is one grand exception to this general rule, and that is, in the case of domestic servants. The same holds, though in less degree, with apprentices and assistant hands; and in less degree only, because, in this last case, the difference of grade is slighter. Domestic servants and assistants in business and trade, come most closely and continually into contact with their employers; they are about them from morning to night, see them in every phase of character, in every style of humour, in every act of life. How *influence will descend!* Conscientiousness is spread, not only by precept but by example, and, so to speak, by contagion, it is spread more widely. Kindness is communicated in the same way. Virtue of every kind acts like an electric shock. Those in contact with its practisers receive the communication of it. The same with qualities and tempers that do no honour to our nature. If servants come to you bad, you may at least improve them; possibly almost change their nature. Here follows, then, a receipt to that effect: – *Recipe for obtaining good servants.* – Let them observe in your conduct to others just the qualities and virtues that you would desire they should possess and practise as respects you. Be uniformly kind and gentle. If you reprove, do so with reason and with temper. Be respectable, and you will be respected by him. Be kind, and you will meet kindness from them. Consider their interests, and they will consider yours. A friend in a servant is no contemptible thing. Be to every servant a friend; and heartless, indeed, will be the servant who does not warm in love to you.

TO KILL COCKROACHES – A teacupful of well-bruised Plaster of Paris, mixed with double the quantity of oatmeal, to which add a little sugar (the latter is not essential). Strew it on the floor or in the chinks where they frequent.

WHEN TO CHANGE THE WATER IN WHICH LEECHES ARE KEPT – Once a month in winter, and once a week in summer, is sufficiently often, unless the water becomes discoloured or bloody, when it should be changed every day. Either clean pond water, or clean rain-water should be employed.

PEAS PUDDING – Dry a pint or quart of split peas thoroughly before the fire; then tie them up loosely in a cloth, put them into warm water, boil them a couple of hours, or more, until quite tender; take them up, beat them well in a dish with a little salt, (some add the yolk of an egg,) and a bit of butter. Make it quite smooth, tie it up again in a cloth, and boil it an hour longer. This is highly nourishing.

TO CLEAR VEGETABLES OF INSECTS – Make a strong brine of one pound and a half of salt to one gallon of water, into this place the vegetables with the stalk ends uppermost, for two or three hours; this will destroy all the insects which cluster in the leaves, and they will fall out and sink to the bottom of the water.

TO PREVENT MICE TAKING PEAS – Previous to the peas being sown, they should be well saturated with a solution of bitter aloes; or, they may be saturated with salad oil, and then rolled in some powdered resin previous to sowing, and the mice will not touch them.

DEVONSHIRE JUNCKET – Put warm milk into a bowl, turn it with a little rennet, then add some scalded cream, sugar, and cinnamon on the top, without breaking the curd.

CHLOROFORMING BEES – The quantity of chloroform required for an ordinary hive is the sixth part of an ounce; a very large hive may take nearly a quarter of an ounce. Set down a table opposite to, and about four feet distant from the hive; on the table spread a thick linen cloth, in the centre of the table place a small shallow breakfast plate, covered with a piece of wire gauze, to prevent the bees from coming in immediate contact with the chloroform. Now quickly and cautiously lift the hive from the board on which it is standing, set it down on the top of the table, keeping the plate in the centre; cover the hive closely up with cloths, and in twenty minutes or so the bees are not only sound asleep, but not one is left among the combs; the whole of them are lying helpless on the table. You now remove what honey you think fit, replace the hive in its old stand, and the bees, as they recover, will return to their domicile. A bright, calm, sunny day is the best; and you should commence your operations early in the morning, before many of them are abroad.

ARNICA FOR BITES – A correspondent of the *Times* says: – "Noticing in your paper an account of the death of a man from the bite of a cat, I beg to trouble you with the following case, which occurred to myself about three weeks ago: – I took a strange dog home, which produced consternation among the cats. One of them I took up, to effect a reconciliation between her and the dog. In her terror she bit me so severely on the first finger of the left hand, as not only to cause four of the teeth of her lower jaw to enter the flesh, but so agonising was her bite that the pressure of her palate caused the finger to swell at the joint on the opposite side to where the lower teeth entered the finger. In a minute or two the pain was about as excruciating as anything I ever felt – certainly greater than I have suffered from a wound. I got some tincture of arnica, diluted with about twelve times the quantity of water, and proceeded to bathe the finger well with it. In about half a minute the blood began to flow freely, the pain ceased, and the swelling abated, and up to this moment I have had no further inconvenience nor pain, not even soreness.

A VERY PLEASANT PERFUME, and also preventive against moths, may be made of the following ingredients: – Take of cloves, caraway seeds, nutmeg, mace, cinnamon, and Tonquin beans, of each one ounce; then add as much Florentine orris-root as will equal the other ingredients put together. Grind the whole well to powder, and then put it in little bags, among your clothes, &c.

DESTRUCTION OF RATS – The following recipe for the destruction of rats has been communicated by Dr. Ure to the council of the English Agricultural Society, and is highly recommended as the best known means of getting rid of these most obnoxious and destructive vermin. It has been tried by several intelligent persons, and found perfectly effectual. – Melt hog's lard in a bottle plunged in water, heated to about 150 degrees of Fahrenheit; introduce into it half an ounce of phosphorus for every pound of lard; then add a pint of proof-spirit or whiskey; cork the bottle firmly after its contents have been heated to 150 degrees, taking it at the same time out of the water, and agitate smartly till the phosphorus becomes uniformly diffused, forming a milky-looking liquid. This liquid, being cooled, will afford a white compound of phosphorus and lard, from which the spirit spontaneously separates, and may be poured off to be used again, for none of it enters into the combination, but it merely serves to comminute the phosphorus, and diffuse it in very fine particles through the lard. This compound, on being warmed very gently, may be poured out into a mixture of wheat flour and sugar, incorporated therewith, and then flavoured with oil of rhodium, or not, at pleasure. The flavour may be varied with oil of aniseed, &c. This dough, being made into pellets, is to be laid in rat-holes. By its luminousness in the dark, it attracts their notice, and being agreeable to their palates and noses, it is readily eaten, and proves certainly fatal.

PHOSPHORUS PASTE FOR DESTROYING RATS AND MICE – Melt one pound of lard with a very gentle heat in a bottle or glass flask plunged into warm water; then add half an ounce of phosphorus, and one pint of proof spirit; cork the bottle securely, and as it cools shake it frequently, so as to mix the phosphorus uniformly; when cold pour off the spirit (which may be preserved for the same purpose), and thicken the mixture with flour. Small portions of this mixture may be placed near the rat holes, and being luminous in the dark it attracts them, is eaten greedily, and is certainly fatal. N.B. There is no danger of fire from its use. Cost: phosphorus, 6d. per ounce; lard, 1s. per pound.

TO DESTROY ANTS – Drop some quicklime on the mouth of their nest, and wash it in with boiling water; or dissolve some camphor in spirits of wine, then mix with water, and pour into their haunts; or tobacco water, which has been found effectual. They are averse to strong scents. Camphor will prevent their infesting a cupboard, or a sponge saturated with creosote. To prevent their climbing up trees, place a ring of tar about the trunk, or a circle of rag moistened occasionally with creosote.

SLUGS AND SNAILS are great enemies to every kind of garden-plant, whether flower or vegetable; they wander in the night to feed, and return at day-light to their haunts; the shortest and surest direction is, "rise early, catch them, and kill them." If you are an early riser, you may cut them off from their day retreats, or you may lay cabbage leaves about the ground, especially on the beds which they frequent. Every

morning examine these leaves, and you will find a great many taking refuge beneath; if they plague you very much, search for their retreat, which you can find by their slimy track, and hunt there for them day by day; lime and salt are very annoying to snails and slugs; a pinch of salt kills them, and they will not touch fresh lime; it is a common practice to sprinkle lime over young crops, and along the edges of beds, about rows of peas and beans, lettuces and other vegetables; but when it has been on the ground some days, or has been moistened by rain, it loses its strength.

CATERPILLARS AND APHIDES – A garden syringe or engine, with a cap on the pipe full of very minute holes, will wash away these disagreeable visitors very quickly. You must bring the pipe close to the plant, and pump hard, so as to have considerable force on, and the plant, however badly infested, will soon be cleared without receiving any injury. Every time that you use the syringe or garden engine, you must immediately rake the earth under the trees, and kill the insects you have dislodged, or many will recover and climb up the stems of the plants.

GRUBS on orchard-trees and gooseberry and currant bushes, will sometimes be sufficiently numerous to spoil a crop; but, if a bonfire be made with dry sticks and weeds on the windward side of the orchard, so that the smoke may blow among the trees, you will destroy thousands; for the grubs have such an objection to smoke, that very little of it makes them roll themselves up and fall off; they must be swept up afterwards.

WASPS destroy a good deal of fruit, but every pair of wasps killed in spring saves the trouble and annoyance of a swarm in autumn; it is necessary, however, to be very careful in any attempt upon a wasp, for its sting is painful and lasting. In case of being stung, get the blue bag from the laundry, and rub it well into the wound as soon as possible. Later in the season, it is customary to hang vessels of beer, or water and sugar, in the fruit-trees, to entice them to drown themselves.

BUTTERFLIES AND MOTHS, however pretty, are the worst enemies one can have in a garden; a single insect of this kind may deposit eggs enough to overrun a tree with caterpillars, therefore they should be destroyed at any cost of trouble. The only moth that you must spare, is the common black and red one; the grubs of this feed exclusively on groundsel, and are therefore a valuable ally of the gardener.

EARWIGS are very destructive insects; their favourite food is the petals of roses, pinks, dahlias, and other flowers. They may be caught by driving stakes into the ground, and placing on each an inverted flower pot; the earwigs will climb up and take refuge under it, when they may be taken out and killed. Clean bowls of tobacco-pipes placed in like manner on the tops of smaller sticks are very good traps; or very deep holes may be made in the ground with a crowbar, into these they will fall, and may be destroyed by boiling water.

TOADS are among the best friends the gardener has; for they live almost exclusively on the most destructive kinds of vermin. Unsightly, therefore, though they may be, they should on all accounts be encouraged; they should never be touched nor molested in any way; on the contrary, places of shelter should be made for them, to which they may retire from the burning heat of the sun. If you have none in your garden, it will be quite worth your while to search for them in your walks, and bring them home, taking care to handle them tenderly, for although they have neither the will nor the power to injure you, a very little rough treatment will injure them; no cucumber or melon frame should be without one or two. - *Glenny's Gardening for Children*.

GARDENING OPERATIONS FOR THE YEAR

JANUARY - *Flower of the month* - Christmas Rose.

Indoor preparations for future operations must be made, as in this month there are only five hours a-day available for out-door work, unless the season be unusually mild. Mat over tulip-beds, begin to force roses. Pot over secale and plant dried roots of border flowers in mild weather. Take strawberries in pots into the green-house. Prune and plant gooseberry, currant, fruit and deciduous trees and shrubs. Cucumbers and melons to be sown in the hot bed. Apply manures.

FEBRUARY – *Flowers of the month* – Snowdrop and violet.

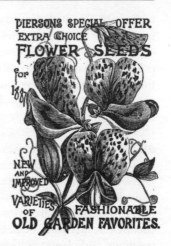

Transplant pinks, carnations, sweet-williams, candituft, campanulas, &c., sweet and garden peas and lettuce, for succession of crops, covering the ground with straw, &c. Sow also savoys, leeks and cabbages. Prune and nail walnut trees, and towards the end of the month plant stocks for next year's grafting, also cuttings of poplar, elder, willow-trees, for ornamental shrubbery. Sow fruit and forest tree seeds.

MARCH – *Flower of the month* – Primrose.

"Spring flowers" to be sown. Border flowers to be planted out. Tender annuals to be potted out under glasses. Mushroom beds to be made. *Sow* artichokes, windsor beans, and cauliflowers for autumn; lettuces and peas for succession of crops, onions, parsley, radishes, savoys, asparagus, red and white cabbages, and beets; turnips, early broccoli, parsnips and carrots. Plant slips and parted roots of perennial herbs. Graft trees and protect early blossoms. Force rose-tree cuttings under glasses.

APRIL – *Flower of the month* – Cowslip.

Sow for succession peas, beans and carrots; parsnips, celery and secale. Sow "Spring flowers." Plant evergreens, dahlias, chrysan-themums, and the like, also potatoes, slips of thyme, parted roots, lettuces, cauliflowers, cabbages, onions. Lay down turf, remove caterpillars. Sow and graft Camellias, and propagate and graft fruit and rose trees by all the various means in use. Sow cucumbers and vegetable marrows for planting out. *This is the most important month in the year for gardeners.*

MAY – *Flower of the month* – Hawthorn.

Plant out your seedling flowers as they are ready, and sow again for succession larkspur, mignionette, and other spring flowers. Pot out tender annuals. Remove auriculas to a N.E. aspect. Take up bulbous roots as the leaves decay. Sow kidney beans, broccoli for spring use, cape for autumn, cauliflowers for December; Indian corn, cress, onions, to plant out as bulbs next year, radishes, aromatic herbs, turnips, cabbages, savoys, lettuces, &c. Plant celery, lettuces, and annuals; thin spring crops. Stick peas, &c. Earth up potatoes, &c. Moisten mushroom beds.

JUNE – *Flowers of the month* – Waterlily, Honeysuckle.

Sow giant stocks to flower next spring. *Slip* myrtles to strike, and *lay* pinks, carnations, roses, and evergreens. *Plant* annuals in borders, and auriculas in shady places. Sow kidney beans, pumpkins, cucumbers for pickling, and (late in the month) endive and lettuces. Plant out cucumbers, marrows, leeks, celery, broccoli, cauliflowers, savoys, and seedlings, and plants propagated by slips. Earth up potatoes, &c. Cut herbs for drying when in flower.

JULY – *Flowers of the Month* – Rose and carnation.

Part auricula and polyanthus roots. Take up summer bulbs as they go out of flower, and plant saffron crocus and autumn bulbs. Gather seeds. Clip evergreen borders and hedges, strike myrtle slips under glasses. Net fruit trees. Finish budding by the end of the month. Head down espaliers. Sow early dwarf cabbages to plant out in October for spring; also endive, onions, kidney beans for late crop, and turnips. Plant celery, endive, lettuces, cabbages, leeks, strawberries, and cauliflowers. Stick peas. Tie up salads. Earth celery. Take up onions, &c., for drying.

AUGUST – *Flowers of the Month* – Harebell and mallow.

Sow flowers to flower in-doors in winter, and pot all young stocks raised in the greenhouse. Sow early red cabbages, cauliflowers for spring and summer use, cos and cabbage lettuce for winter crop. Plant out winter crops. Dry herbs and mushroom spawn.

Plant out strawberry roots, and net currant trees, to preserve the fruit through the winter.

SEPTEMBER – *Flowers of the Month* – Clematis, or traveller's joy, arbutus, and meadow saffron.

Plant crocuses, scaly bulbs, and evergreen shrubs. Propagate by layers and cuttings of all herbaceous plants, currant, gooseberry, and other fruit trees. Plant out seedling pinks. Sow onions for spring plantation, carrots, spinach, and Spanish radishes in warm spots. Earth up celery. House potatoes and edible bulbs. Gather pickling cucumbers. Make tulip and mushroom beds.

OCTOBER – *Flowers of the Month* – China-aster, holly, and ivy.

Sow rose-tree seeds and fruit stones, also larkspurs and the hardier annuals to stand the winter, also hyacinths and smooth bulbs, in pots and glasses. Plant young trees, cuttings of jasmine, honeysuckle, and evergreens. Sow mignionette for pots in winter. Plant cabbages, &c., for spring. Cut down asparagus, separate roots of daisies, irises, &c. Trench, drain, and manure.

NOVEMBER – *Flowers of the month* – Laurestine and Wych Hazel.

Sow sweet peas for an early crop. Take up dahlia roots. Complete beds for asparagus and artichokes. Plant dried roots of border flowers, daisies, &c. Take potted-mignionette in-doors. Set strawberries. Sow peas, leeks, beans, and radishes. Plant rhubarb in rows. Prune hardy trees, and plant stocks of fruit trees. Store carrots, &c. Shelter from frost where it may be required. Plant shrubs for forcing. Continue to trench and manure vacant ground.

DECEMBER – *Flowers of the month* – Cyclamen and Winter aconite. (Holly berries are now available for floral decoration.)

Continue in open weather to prepare vacant ground for spring, and to protect plants from frost. Cover bulbous roots with matting. Dress flower borders. Prepare forcing ground for cucumbers, and force asparagus and secale. Plant goose-berry, currant, apple and pear trees. Roll grass plats if the season be mild and not too wet. Prepare poles, stakes, pea-sticks, &c., for spring.

KITCHEN GARDEN – This is one of the most important parts of general domestic economy, whenever the situation of a house will permit a family to avail themselves of its assistance, in aid of butchers' bills. It is, indeed, much to be regretted that small plots of ground, in the immediate vicinity of the metropolis more especially, are too often frittered away into shrubberies and baby gardens, when they might more usefully be employed in raising vegetables for the family, during the week-day residence in town, than wasting their sweetness on the smoky air in all the pride of lilac, hollyhock, and bachelors' buttons, to be merely smelled to, by the whole immigrating household on the day of rest. With a little care and attention, a kitchen-garden, though small, might be rendered not only useful, but, in fact, as ornamental as a modern grass carpet; and the same expense incurred to make the ground a labyrinth of sweets, might suffice to render it agreeable to the palate, as well as to the olfactory nerves, and that even without offending the most delicate optics. It is only in accordance with our plan to give the hint, and to record such novel points as may facilitate the proposed arrangement. It is one objection to the adoption of a kitchen-garden in front of the dwelling, or in sight of the family apartments, that its very nature makes it rather an eye-sore than otherwise at all seasons. This, however, is an objection that may be readily got over by a little attention to neatness and good order, whilst the plants themselves, if judiciously attended to, and the borders sown or planted with ranunculus, polyanthus, mignionette, &c., in succession, will really be ornamental: but then, in cutting the plants for use, the business must be done neatly, all useless leaves cleared from the ground, the roots no longer wanted taken up, and the ravages of insects to be guarded against by sedulous extirpation. It will also be found a great improvement, where space will admit of it, to surround the beds with neat espaliers, with fruit trees, or even gooseberry and currant bushes trained along them, instead of these being suffered to grow in a state of ragged wildness.

COLLECTING AND LAYING OUT SEA-WEEDS – First wash the sea-weed in fresh water, then take a plate, or dish (the larger the better), cut your paper to the size required, place it in the plate with fresh water, and spread out the plant with a good-sized camel-hair pencil in a natural form (picking out with the pin gives the sea-weed an unnatural appearance, and destroys the characteristic fall of the branches, which should be carefully avoided); then gently raise the paper with the specimen out of the water, placing it in a slanting position for a few moments, so as to allow the super-abundant water to run off; after which, place it in the press. The press is made with either three pieces of board or paste-board. Lay on the first board two sheets of blotting-paper; on that lay your specimens; place straight and smooth over them a piece of old muslin, fine cambric, or linen; then some more blotting-paper, and place another board on the top of that, and continue in the same way. The blotting-paper and the muslin should be carefully removed and dried every day, and then replaced; at the same time, those specimens that are sufficiently dried may be taken away. Nothing now remains but to write on each the name, date, and locality. You can either gum the specimens in a scrap-book, or fix them in, as drawings are often fastened, by making four slits in the page, and inserting each corner. This is by far the best plan, as it admits of their removal, without injury to the page, at any future period, if it be required either to insert better specimens, or intermediate species. Some of the larger Algae will not adhere to the paper, and consequently require gumming. The following method of preserving them has been communicated to me by a botanical friend: – "After well cleaning and pressing, brush the coarser kinds of Algae over with spirits of turpentine, in which two or three small lumps of gum mastic have been dissolved, by shaking in a warm place; two-thirds of a small phial is the proper proportion, and this will make the specimens retain a fresh appearance." – *Miss Gifford's Marine Botanist*.

DRY BOTANICAL SPECIMENS FOR PRESERVATION – The plants you wish to preserve should be gathered when the weather is dry, and after placing the ends in water, let them remain in a cool place till the next day. When about to be submitted to the process of drying, place each plant between several sheets of blotting-paper, and iron it with a large smooth heater, pretty strongly warmed, till all the moisture is dissipated. Colours may thus be fixed, which otherwise become pale, or nearly white. Some plants require more moderate heat than others, and herein consists the nicety of the experiment; but I have generally found, that if the iron be not too hot, and is passed rapidly, yet carefully, over the surface of the blotting paper it answers the purpose equally well with plants of almost every variety of hue and thickness. In compound flowers, with those also of a stubborn and solid form, as the Centaurea, some little art is required in cutting away the under part, by which means the profile and forms of the flowers will be more distinctly exhibited. This is especially necessary, when the method employed by Major Velley is adopted; viz., to fix the flowers and fructification down with gum upon the paper previous to ironing, by which means they become almost incorporated with the surface. When this very delicate process is attempted, blotting-paper should be laid under every part excepting the blossoms, in order to prevent staining the white paper. Great care must be taken to keep preserved specimens in a dry place.

SKELETON LEAVES may be made by steeping leaves in rain water, in an open vessel, exposed to the air and sun. Water must occasionally be added to compensate loss by evaporation. The leaves will putrefy, and then their membranes will begin to open; then lay them on a clean white plate, filled with clean water, and with gentle touches take off the external membranes, separating them cautiously near the middle rib. When there is an opening towards the latter the whole membrane separates easily. The process requires a great deal of patience, as ample time must be given for the vegetable tissues to decay, and separate.

A MORE EXPEDITIOUS METHOD – A tablespoonful of chloride of lime in a liquid state, mixed with a quart of pure spring water. Leaves or seed vessels of plants to be soaked in the mixture for about four hours, then taken out and well washed in a large basin filled with water, after which, they should be left to dry with free exposure to light and air. Some of the larger species of forest leaves, or such as have strong ribs, will require to be left rather more than four hours in the liquid.

THE CHEMICAL BAROMETER – Take a long narrow bottle, such as an old-fashioned Eau-de-Cologne bottle, and put into it two and a-half drachms of camphor, and eleven drachms of spirits of wine; when the camphor is dissolved, which it will readily do by slight agitation, add the following mixture: – Take water, nine drachms: nitrate of potash (saltpetre), thirty-eight grains; and muriate of ammonia (sal ammoniac), thirty-eight grains. Dissolve these salts in the water prior to mixing with the camphorated spirit; then shake the whole well together. Cork the bottle well, and wax the top, but afterwards make a very small aperture in the cork with a red-hot needle. The bottle may then be hung up, or placed in any stationary position. By observing the different appearances which the materials assume, as the weather changes, it becomes an excellent prognosticator of a coming storm or of a sunny sky.

Home Remedies

BATHING – If to preserve health be to save medical expenses, without even reckoning upon time and comfort, there is no part of the household arrangement so important to the domestic economist as cheap convenience for personal ablution. For this purpose baths upon a large and expensive scale are by no means necessary; but though temporary or tin baths may be extremely useful upon pressing occasions, it will be found to be finally as cheap, and much more readily convenient, to have a permanent bath constructed, which may be done in any dwelling-house of moderate size, without interfering with other general purposes. As the object of these remarks is not to present essays, but merely useful economic hints, it is unnecessary to expatiate upon the architectural arrangement of the bath, or, more properly speaking, the bathing-place, which may be fitted up for the most retired establishment, differing in size or shape agreeable to the spare room that may be appropriated to it, and serving to exercise both the fancy and the judgment in its preparation. Nor is it particularly necessary to notice the salubrious effects resulting from the bath, beyond the two points of its being so conducive both to health and cleanliness, in keeping up a free circulation of the blood, without any violent muscular exertion, thereby really affording a saving of strength, and producing its effects without any expense either to the body or to the purse.

WHOEVER FITS UP A BATH in a house already built must be guided by circumstances; but it will always be proper to place it as near the kitchen fire-place as possible, because from thence it may be heated, or at least have its temperature preserved by means of hot air through tubes, or by steam prepared by the culinary fireplace, without interfering with its ordinary uses.

TO SOFTEN THE SKIN, AND IMPROVE THE COMPLEXION – If flowers of sulphur be mixed in a little of milk, and after standing an hour or two, the milk (without disturbing the sulphur) be rubbed into the skin, it will keep it soft, and make the complexion clear.

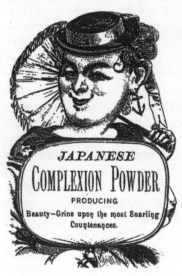

JAPANESE
COMPLEXION POWDER
PRODUCING
Beauty–Grins upon the most Snarling
Countenances.

It is to be used before washing. A lady of our acquaintance, being exceedingly anxious about her complexion, adopted the above suggestion. In about a fortnight she wrote to us to say that the mixture became so disagreeable after it had been made a few days, that she could not use it. We should have wondered if she could – the milk became putrid! A little of the mixture should have been prepared over night with evening milk, and used the next morning, but not afterwards. About a wine-glassful made for each occasion would suffice.

THE HANDS – Take a wine-glassful of eau de Cologne, and another of lemon-juice: then scrape two cakes of brown Windsor soap to a powder, and mix well in a mould. When hard, it will be an excellent soap for whitening the hands.

TO WHITEN THE NAILS – Diluted sulphuric acid, two drachms; tincture of myrrh, one drachm; spring water, four ounces; mix. First cleanse with white soap, and then dip the fingers into the mixture.

EYELASHES – The mode adopted by the beauties of the East to increase the length and strength of their eyelashes is simply to clip the split ends with a pair of scissors about once a month. Mothers perform the operation on their children, both male and female, when they are mere infants, watching the opportunity whilst they sleep; the practice never fails to produce the desired effect. We recommend it to the attention of our fair readers, as a safe and innocent means of enhancing the charms which so many of them, no doubt, already possess.

BITING THE NAILS – This is a habit that should be immediately corrected in children, as, if persisted in for any length of time, it permanently deforms the nails. Dipping the finger-ends in some bitter tincture will generally prevent children from putting them to the mouth; but if this fails, as it sometimes will, each finger-end ought to be encased in a stall until the propensity is eradicated.

TO FILL A DECAYED TOOTH – Procure a 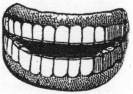 small piece of gutta percha, drop it into boiling water, then, with the thumb and finger, take off as much as you suppose will fill up the tooth nearly level, and while in this soft state press it into the tooth; then hold on that side of the mouth cold water two or three times, which will harden it.

TO RESTORE HAIR WHEN REMOVED BY ILL HEALTH OR AGE – Onions rubbed frequently on the part requiring it. The stimulating powers of this vegetable are of service in restoring the tone of the skin, and assisting the capillary vessels in sending forth new hair; but it is not infallible. Should it succeed, however, the growth of these new hairs may be assisted by the oil of myrtle-berries, the repute of which, perhaps, is greater than its real efficacy. These applications are cheap and harmless, even where they do no good; a character which cannot be said of the numerous quack remedies that meet the eye in every direction.

SCURF IN THE HEAD – A simple and effectual remedy. Into a pint of water drop a lump of fresh quick lime, the size of a walnut; let it stand all night, then pour the water off clear from sediment or deposit, add a quarter of a pint of the best vinegar, and wash the head with the mixture. Perfectly harmless; only wet the roots of the hair.

HICCOUGH OR HICCUP – This is a spasm of the diaphragm, caused by flatulency, indigestion, or acidity. It may be relieved by the sudden application of cold, also by two or three mouthfuls of cold water, by eating a small piece of ice, taking a pinch of snuff, or anything that excites counter action.

SORE THROAT – I have been subject to sore throat, and have invariably found the following preparation (simple and cheap) highly efficacious when used in the early stage: Pour a pint of boiling-water upon twenty-five or thirty leaves of common sage; let the infusion stand for half an hour. Add vinegar sufficient to make it moderately acid, and honey according to the taste. This combination of the astringent and the emollient principle seldom fails to produce the desired effect. The infusion

must be used as a gargle several times a day. It has this advantage over many gargles – it is pleasant to the taste, and may be swallowed occasionally, not only without danger, but with advantage.

PAINS IN THE HEAD AND FACE – A friend assures us that he was cured of a severe attack of tic doloreux by the following simple remedy: – Take half a pint of rose water, add two teaspoonfuls of white vinegar, to form a lotion. Apply it to the part affected three or four times a day. It requires fresh linen and lotion each application; this will, in two or three days, gradually take the pain away. The above receipt I feel desirous of being made known to the public, as I have before mentioned the relief I have experienced, and others, whose names I could give. The last remark is our friend's own. We doubt the cure of real tic doloreux by these means; but in many cases of nervous pains the above would be useful, and may easily be tried.

TO AVOID CATCHING A COLD – Accustom yourself to the use of sponging with cold water every morning on first getting out of bed. It should be followed with a good deal of rubbing with a wet towel. It has considerable effect in giving tone to the skin, and maintaining a proper action in it, and thus proves a safeguard to the injurious influence of cold and sudden changes of temperature. Sir Astley Cooper said, "The methods by which I have preserved my own health are – temperance, early rising, and sponging the body every morning with cold water, immediately after getting out of bed; a practice which I have adopted for thirty years without ever catching cold."

UTILITY OF SINGING – It is asserted, and we believe with some truth, that singing is a corrective of the common tendency to pulmonic complaints. Dr. Rush, an eminent physician, observes on this subject: – "'The Germans are seldom afflicted with consumption; and this, I believe, is in part occasioned by the strength which their lungs acquire by exercising them in vocal music, for this constitutes an essential branch of their education. The music master of an academy has furnished me with a remark still more in favour of this opinion. He informed me that he had known several instances of persons who were strongly disposed to consumption, who were restored to health by the exercise of their lungs in singing."

RULES FOR THE PRESERVATION OF HEALTH

PURE ATMOSPHERIC AIR is composed of nitrogen, oxygen, and a *very* small proportion of carbonic acid gas. Air once breathed has lost the chief part of its oxygen, and acquired a proportionate increase of carbonic acid gas.

THEREFORE, health requires that we breathe the same air once only.

THE SOLID PARTS of our bodies are continually wasting, and require to be repaired by fresh substances.

THEREFORE, food, which is to repair the loss, should be taken with due regard to the exercise and waste of the body.

THE FLUID PART of our bodies also wastes constantly; there is but one fluid in animals, which is water.

THEREFORE, water only is necessary, and no artifice can produce a better drink.

THE FLUID of our bodies is to the solid in proportion as nine to one.

THEREFORE, a like proportion should prevail in the total amount of food taken.

LIGHT exercises an important influence upon the growth and vigour of animals and plants.

THEREFORE, our dwellings should freely admit the solar rays.

DECOMPOSING ANIMAL AND VEGETABLE SUBSTANCES yield various noxious gases, which enter the lungs and corrupt the blood.

THEREFORE, all impurities should be kept away from our abodes, and every precaution be observed to secure a pure atmosphere.

WARMTH is essential to all the bodily functions.

THEREFORE, an equal bodily temperature should be maintained by exercise, by clothing, or by fire.

EXERCISE warms, invigorates, and purifies the body; clothing preserves the warmth the body generates; fire imparts warmth externally.

THEREFORE, to obtain and preserve warmth, exercise and clothing are preferable to fire.

FIRE consumes the oxygen of the air, and produces noxious gases.

THEREFORE, the air is less pure in the presence of candles, gas, or coal fire, than otherwise, and the deterioration should be repaired by increased ventilation.

THE SKIN is a highly-organised membrane, full of minute pores, cells, blood-vessels, and nerves; it imbibes moisture or throws it off, according to the state of the atmosphere and the temperature of the body. It also "breathes," as do the lungs (though less actively). All the internal organs sympathise with the skin.

THEREFORE, it should be repeatedly cleansed.

LATE HOURS and anxious pursuits exhaust the nervous system, and produce disease and premature death.

THEREFORE, the hours of labour and study should be short.

MENTAL AND BODILY EXERCISE are equally essential to the general health and happiness.

THEREFORE, labour and study should succeed each other.

MAN will live most healthily upon simple solids and fluids, of which a sufficient but temperate quantity should be taken.

THEREFORE, strong drinks, tobacco, snuff, opium, and all mere indulgences should be avoided.

SUDDEN ALTERNATIONS OF HEAT AND COLD are dangerous (especially to the young and the aged).

THEREFORE, clothing, in quantity and quality, should be adapted to the alterations of night and day, and of the seasons.

AND, THEREFORE, ALSO, drinking cold water when the body is hot, and hot tea and soups when cold, are productive of many evils.

MODERATION in eating and drinking, short hours of labour and study, regularity in exercise, recreation, and rest, cleanliness, equanimity of temper and equality of temperature, these are the great essentials to that which surpasses all wealth, *health of mind and body*.

CAUTIONS FOR THE PREVENTION OF ACCIDENTS

The following regulations should be engraved on the memories of all: –

AS MOST SUDDEN DEATHS come by water, particular caution is therefore necessary in its vicinity.

STAND NOT NEAR A TREE, or any leaden spout, iron gate, or palisade, in time of lightning.

LAY LOADED GUNS IN SAFE PLACES, and never imitate firing a gun in jest.

NEVER SLEEP NEAR CHARCOAL; if drowsy at any work where charcoal fires are used, take the fresh air.

WHEN BENUMBED WITH cold beware of sleeping out of doors; rub yourself, if you have it in your power, with snow, and do not hastily approach the fire.

AIR VAULTS, by letting them remain open some time before you enter, or scattering powdered lime in them. Where a lighted candle will not burn, animal life cannot exist; it will be an excellent caution, therefore, before entering damp and confined places, to try this simple experiment.

NEVER LEAVE SADDLE OR DRAUGHT HORSES, while in use, by themselves; nor go immediately behind a led horse as he is apt to kick.

BE WARY OF CHILDREN, whether they are up or in bed; and particularly when they are near the fire, an element with which they are very apt to amuse themselves.

LEAVE NOTHING POISONOUS open or accessible; and never omit to write the word "Poison" in large letters upon it, wherever it may be placed.

IN WALKING THE STREETS keep out of the line of the cellars, and never look one way and walk another.

NEVER THROW PIECES of orange-peel, or broken glass bottles into the streets.

NEVER MEDDLE with gunpowder by candle-light.

IN TRIMMING A LAMP WITH NAPTHA, never fill it. Leave space for the spirit to expand with warmth.

WHEN THE BRASS ROD of the stair-carpet becomes loose, fasten it immediately.

IN OPENING EFFERVESCING DRINKS, such as soda water, hold the cork in your hand.

QUIT YOUR HOUSE WITH CARE on a frosty morning.

HAVE YOUR HORSES' shoes roughed directly there are indications of frost.

CAUTIONS IN VISITING THE SICK – Do not visit the sick when you are fatigued, or when in a state of perspiration, or with the stomach empty – for in such conditions you are liable to take the infection. When the disease is very contagious, take the side of the patient which is near to the window. Do not enter the room the first thing in the morning before it has been aired; and when you come away, take some food, change your clothing immediately, and expose the latter to the air for some days. Tobacco-smoke is a preventive of malaria.

ICELAND MOSS CHOCOLATE FOR THE SICK ROOM – Iceland moss has been in the highest repute on the continent as a most efficacious remedy in incipient pulmonary complaints; combined with chocolate, it will be found a nutritious article of diet, and may be taken as a morning and evening beverage. – *Directions:* – Mix a teaspoonful of the chocolate with a teaspoonful of boiling water or milk, stirring it constantly until it is completely dissolved.

LEECHES AND THEIR APPLICATION – The leech used for medical purposes is called the *Hirudo Medicinalis*, to distinguish it from other varieties, such as the horse-leech and the Lisbon leech. It varies from two to four inches in length, and is of a blackish brown colour, marked on the back with six yellow spots, and edged with a yellow line on each side. Formerly leeches were supplied by Lincolnshire, Yorkshire, and other fenny countries, but latterly most of the leeches are procured from France, where they are now becoming scarce.

WHEN LEECHES ARE APPLIED TO A PART, it should be thoroughly freed from down or hair by shaving, and all liniments, &c. carefully and effectually cleaned away by washing. If the leech is hungry it will soon bite, but sometimes great difficulty is experienced in getting them to fasten on. When this is the case, roll the leech into a little porter, or moisten the surface with a little blood, or milk, or sugar and water. Leeches may be applied by holding them over the part with a piece of linen cloth, or by means of an inverted glass, under which they must be placed.

WHEN APPLIED TO THE GUMS, care should be taken to use a leech glass, as they are apt to creep down the patient's throat; a large swan's quill will answer the purpose of a leech glass. When leeches are gorged they will drop off themselves; never *tear* them off from a person, but just dip the point of a moistened finger into some salt and touch them with it.

LEECHES are supposed to abstract about two drachms of blood, or six leeches draw about an ounce; but this is independent of the bleeding after they have come off, and more blood generally flows then than during the time they are sucking.

AFTER LEECHES COME AWAY, encourage the bleeding by flannels dipped in hot water and wrung out dry, and then apply a warm "spongio-piline" poultice. If the bleeding is not to be encouraged, cover the bites with rag dipped in olive oil, or spread with spermaceti ointment, having previously sponged the parts clean.

WHEN BLEEDING CONTINUES FROM LEECH BITES, and it is desirable to stop it, apply pressure with the fingers over the part, or dip a rag in a strong solution of alum and lay over them, or use the tincture of sesquichloride of iron, or apply a leaf of matico to them, placing the under surface of the leaf next to the skin, or touch each bite with a finely-pointed piece of lunar caustic; and if all these tried in succession fail, pass a fine needle through a fold of the skin so as to include the bite, and twist a piece of thread round it. Be sure never to allow any one to go to sleep with leech bites bleeding, without watching them carefully; and never apply too many to children.

AFTER LEECHES HAVE BEEN USED they should be placed in water, containing sixteen per cent. of salt, which facilitates the removal of the blood they contain; and they should afterwards be placed one by one in warm water, and the blood forced out by *gentle* pressure. The leeches should then be thrown into fresh water, which is to be renewed every twenty-four hours; and they may then be re-applied after an interval of eight or ten days; a second time they may be disgorged.

IF A LEECH IS ACCIDENTALLY SWALLOWED, or by any means gets into the body, employ an emetic, or enema of salt and water.

LEECH BAROMETER – Take an eight-ounce phial, and put in it three gills of water, and place in it a health leech, changing the water in summer once a week, and in winter once in a fortnight, and it will most accurately prognosticate the weather. If the weather is to be fine, the leech lies motionless at the bottom of the glass, and coiled together in a spiral form; if rain may be expected, it will creep up to the top of its lodgings and remain there till the weather is settled; if we are to have wind, it will move through its habitation with amazing swiftness, and seldom goes to rest till it begins to blow hard; if a remarkable storm of thunder and rain is to succeed, it will lodge for some days before almost continually out of the water, and discover great uneasiness in violent throes and convulsive-like motions; in frost as in clear summer-like weather it lies constantly at the bottom; and in snow as in rainy weather it pitches its dwelling in the very mouth of the phial. The top should be covered over with a piece of muslin.

GERMAN YEAST – We have repeatedly noticed the fatality of late of attacks of carbuncles, and the prevalence of diseases of that nature, which we were disposed to attribute to the state of the atmosphere, and as arising from much the same cause as the visitation of cholera. A correspondent, however, has thrown some  light upon the subject, and we print his statement in the hope that the baking fraternity will be prohibited by law from using the pernicious stuff mentioned. We are protected from the sale of diseased and poisonous meat, and from the adulteration of flour, beer, and other articles, and it is absolutely necessary now that we should be protected from German yeast. Our correspondent says: – "Perhaps not the least important matter on the subject of cookery is to avoid everything calculated to injure the purity of the family bread, whether prepared at home or in the baker's oven, and that this is done to a vast extent (although unconsciously) will be at once apparent from the following statement of facts, upon which the public require to be informed: It is well known that a very large proportion of the bread prepared for family use is raised from what is called German yeast – a noxious compound – imported weekly into Hull in quantities really astounding, and where, I am credibly informed, tons of it are thrown into the sea from having become alive; yet this is used by the great majority of bakers over the kingdom to produce the bread for our vast population, who little suspect the slow poison they are daily and unconsciously consuming, and to which, from discussions in medical societies, and notices in medical journals, it seems extremely probable that the numerous cases of carbuncles and boils, which, within these few years, have proved of so serious and even fatal a character, may owe their origin. It ought to be generally known that this German yeast is prepared from every species of refuse grain, and especially (where they can obtain it) from that which is wholly unfit for the food of either man or beast, and if in a state of positive putrefaction, so much the more valuable it is for their purpose, running the more rapidly and easily into fermentation." The foregoing remarks having appeared in the *Manchester Guardian*, called forth the annexed contradiction in the *Weekly Dispatch*: – "We have received several letters from the yeast importers of the metropolis, complaining of an article copied from the *Manchester Guardian* into the *Dispatch*, and which stated, that the use of German yeast in the fermentation of bread caused carbuncles and boils on the face and body. The great object of the writers is to show that the yeast is perfectly wholesome, and that instead of being manufactured from putrid rye, it is the sediment of the distillation of Hollands, or Scheidam gin, drawn off by a common tap, and compressed into a solid, without any mixture; in fact, the only difference between the brewers' yeast and German yeast is, that the former is a liquid beer yeast, and the latter a spirit yeast compressed. Messers. Wilken and Pugh, the yeast importers, inform us – 'that the Commissioners of her Majesty's Customs have subjected the yeast to analysation, and use it themselves for the purpose of making their own bread, and that her Majesty herself partakes of bread, rolls, &c., fermented by nothing but German yeast.'"

HOW TO MAKE SEA-WATER – There cannot be a question that by far the simplest plan would consist in the evaporation of the sea-water itself in large quantities, preserving the resulting salt in closely-stopped vessels to prevent the absorption of moisture, and vending it in this form to the consumer; the proportion of this dry saline matter being fifty-six ounces to ten gallons of water less three pints. This plan was suggested by Dr. E. Schweitzer, for the extemporaneous formation of sea-water for medicinal baths. Mr. H. Schweitzer writes me that he has for many years made this compound, in accordance with his cousin's analysis. The proportion ordered to be used is six ounces to the gallon of water, and stirred well until dissolved.

CURE FOR BURNS – Of all applications for a burn, we believe that there are none equal to a simple covering of common *wheat-flour*. This is always at hand; and while it requires no skill in using, it produces most astonishing effects. The moisture produced upon the surface of a slight or deep burn is at once absorbed by the flour, and forms a paste which shuts out the air. As long as the fluid matters continue flowing, they are absorbed, and prevented from producing irritation, as they would do if kept from passing off by oily or resinous applications, while the greater the amount of those absorbed by the flour, the thicker the protective covering. Another advantage of the flour covering is, that next to the surface it is kept moist and flexible. It can also be readily washed off, without further irritation in removing. It may occasionally be washed off very carefully, when the crust that it forms has become dry, and a new covering be sprinkled on.

FOR SPRAINS AND BRUISES – Take one pint of train oil, half-a-pound of stone-pitch, half-a-pound of resin, half-a-pound of bees-wax, and half-a-pound of stale tallow, or in like proportion. Boil them together for about half-an-hour, skim off the scum, and pour the liquid into cups, and when cold, it will be ready for use. When needed, it must be spread *as thick, but not thicker*, than blister-salve, upon a piece of coarse flaxen cloth. Apply it to the part sprained or bruised, and let it remain for a day or more; it will give almost immediate relief, and one or two plaisters will be sufficient for a perfect cure.

CURE OF WARTS – Mr. Lawrence, surgeon of St. Bartholomew's, says, the easiest way to get rid of warts is to pare off the thickened skin which covers the prominent wart; cut it off by successive layers; shave it till you come to the surface of the skin, and till you draw blood in two or three places. When you have thus denuded the surface of the skin, rub the part thoroughly over with *lunar caustic*, and one effective operation of this kind will generally destroy the wart; if not, you cut off the black spot which has been occasioned by the caustic, and apply it again; or you may apply *acetic acid*, and thus you will get rid of it.

TO REMOVE FRECKLES – Dissolve, in half an ounce of lemon-juice, one ounce of Venice soap, and add a quarter of an ounce each of oil of bitter almonds, and deliquated oil of tartar. Place this mixture in the sun till it acquires the consistency of ointment. When in this state add three drops of the oil of rhodium, and keep it for use. Apply it to the face and hands in the manner following: Wash the parts at night with elderflower water, then anoint with the ointment. In the morning cleanse the skin from its oily adhesion by washing it copiously in rose water.

COD-LIVER OIL – Cod-liver oil is neither more nor less than cod-oil clarified; and consequently two-thirds of its medicinal qualities are abstracted thereby. Cod-oil can be purchased pure at any wholesale oil warehouse, at about one-thirtieth part of the price charged for the so-called cod-liver oil. Many persons who have used cod-oil pure as imported, have found it to answer much better than the cod-liver oil purchased of a druggist. The best vehicle for taking cod-liver oil in is new milk, and the disagreeable flavour of the drug can easily be covered by the addition of one drachm of orange-peel to every eight ounces of the oil.

CORNS – Boil a potato in its skin, and after it is boiled take the skin and put the inside of it to the corn, and leave it on for about twelve hours; at the end of that period the corn will be much better. The above useful and simple receipt has been tried and found to effect a remedy.

BREATH TAINTED BY ONIONS – Leaves of parsley, eaten with vinegar, will prevent the disagreeable consequences of eating onions.

BUNIONS may be checked in their early development by binding the joint with adhesive plaster, and keeping it on as long as any uneasiness is felt. The bandaging should be perfect, and it might be well to extend it round the foot. An inflamed bunion should be poulticed, and larger shoes be worn. Iodine, twelve grains; lard or spermaceti ointment, half an ounce, makes a capital ointment for bunions. It should be rubbed on gently twice or thrice a-day.

SOFT CORNS may be relieved by placing a small piece of lint between the toes; or be rubbed occasionally with sweet oil.

COL. BIRCH'S RECEIPT for rheumatic gout or acute rheumatism, commonly called the Chelsea Pensioner. – Half an ounce of nitre (saltpetre), half an ounce of sulphur, half an ounce of flower of mustard, half an ounce of Turkey rhubarb, quarter of an ounce of powdered gum guaiacum. Mix. A teaspoonful to be taken every other night for three nights, and omit three nights, in a wine-glassful of cold water, – water which has been well boiled.

OINTMENT FOR THE PILES OR HAEMORRHOIDS – Take of hogs' lard, four ounces, camphor two drachms, powdered galls, one ounce, laudanum, half an ounce. Mix; make an ointment to be applied every night at bed-time.

OINTMENT FOR SORE NIPPLES – Take of tincture of tolu two drachms, spermaceti ointment half an ounce; powdered gum two drachms. Mix. Make an ointment. The white of an egg mixed with brandy is the best application for sore nipples; the person should at the same time use a nipple shield.

DECOCTION OF SARSAPARILLA – Take four ounces of the root, slice it down, put the slices into four pints of water, and simmer for four hours. Take out the sarsaparilla, and beat it into a mash; put it into the liquor again, and boil down to two pints, then strain and cool the liquor. Dose – a wine-glassful three times a-day. Use – to purify the blood after a course of mercury; or, indeed, whenever any taint is given to the constitution, vitiating the blood, and producing eruptive affections.

THE CRIMEAN NIGHTCAP, made in a moment, costing nothing, and admirable for railway and other travellers. – Take your pocket-handkerchief and laying it out the full square, double down *one-third* over the other part. Then raise the whole and turn it over, so that the third folded down shall now be underneath. Then take hold of one of the folded corners, and draw its points towards the centre; then do the same with the other, as in making a cocked-hat, or a boat, of paper. Then take hold of the two remaining corners, and twisting the hem of the handkerchief, continue to roll it until it meets the doubled corners brought to the centre, and catches them up a little. Lift the whole and you will see the form of a cap, which, when applied to the head, will cover the head and ears, and, being tied under the chin, will not come off. Very little practice will enable you to regulate the size of the folds, so as to suit the head.

Food & Drink

CHOICE OF ARTICLES OF FOOD

Nothing is more important in the affairs of housekeeping than the choice of wholesome food. We have been amused by a conundrum which is as follows: – "A man went to market and bought *two* fish. When he reached home he found they were the same as when he had bought them; yet there were *three!*" How was this? The answer is – "He bought two mackerel, and one *smelt!*" Those who envy him his bargain need not care about the following rules; but to others they will be valuable:–

MACKEREL must be perfectly fresh, or it is a very indifferent fish; it will neither bear carriage, nor being kept many hours out of the water. The firmness of the flesh, and the clearness of the eyes, must be the criterion of fresh mackerel, as they are of all other fish.

TURBOT, and all flat white fish, are rigid and firm when fresh; the under side should be of a rich cream colour. When out of season, or too long kept, this becomes a bluish white, and the flesh soft and flaccid. A clear bright eye in fish is also a mark of being fresh and good.

COD is known to be fresh by the rigidity of the muscles (or flesh); the redness of the gills, and clearness of the eyes. Crimping much improves this fish.

SALMON – The flavour and excellence of this fish depends upon its freshness, and the shortness of time since it was caught; for no method can completely preserve the delicate flavour it has when just taken out of the water. A great deal of what is brought to London has been packed in ice, and comes from the Scotch and Irish rivers, and though quite fresh, is not quite equal to Thames salmon.

HERRINGS can only be eaten when very fresh, and, like mackerel, will not remain good many hours after they are caught.

FRESH-WATER FISH – The remarks as to firmness and clear fresh eyes apply to this variety of fish, of which there are carp, tench, pike, perch, &c.

LOBSTERS, recently caught, have always some remains of muscular action in the claws, which may be excited by pressing the eyes with the finger; when this cannot be produced, the lobster must have been too long kept. When boiled, the tail preserves its elasticity if fresh, but loses it as soon as it becomes stale. The heaviest lobsters are the best; when light they are watery and poor. Hen lobsters may generally be known by the spawn, or by the breadth of the "flap."

CRAB AND CRAYFISH must be chosen by observations similar to those given above in the choice of lobsters. Crabs have an agreeable smell when fresh.

PRAWNS AND SHRIMPS, when fresh, are firm and crisp.

OYSTERS – If fresh, the shell is firmly closed; when the shells of oysters are opened, they are dead, and unfit for food. The small-shelled oysters, the Pyfleet, Colchester, and Milford, are the finest in flavour.

Larger kinds, called rock oysters, are generally considered only fit for stewing and sauces, though some persons prefer them.

BEEF – The grain of ox beef, when good, is loose, the meat red, and the fat inclining to yellow. Cow beef, on the contrary, has a closer grain, a whiter fat, but meat scarcely as red as that of ox beef. Inferior beef, which is meat obtained from ill-fed animals, or from those which had become too old for food, may be known by a hard skinny fat, a dark red lean, and, in old animals, a line of horny texture running through the meat of the ribs. When meat pressed by the finger rises up quickly, it may be considered as that of an animal which was in its prime; when the dent made by pressure returns slowly, or remains visible, the animal had probably past its prime, and the meat consequently must be of inferior quality.

VEAL should be delicately white, though it is often juicy and well flavoured when rather dark in colour. Butchers, it is said, bleed calves purposely before killing them, with a view to make the flesh white, but this also makes it dry and flavourless. On examining the loin, if the fat enveloping the kidney be white and firm-looking, the meat will probably be prime and recently killed. Veal will not keep so long as an older meat, especially in hot or damp weather; when going, the fat becomes soft, and moist, the meat flabby and spotted, and somewhat porous, like sponge. Large overgrown veal is inferior to small, delicate, yet fat veal. The fillet of a cow-calf is known by the udder attached to it, and by the softness of the skin; it is preferable to the veal of a bull-calf.

MUTTON – The meat should be firm and close in grain, and red in colour, the fat white and firm. Mutton is in its prime when the sheep is about five years old, though it is often killed much younger. If too young, the flesh feels tender when pinched; if too old, on being pinched, it wrinkles up, and so remains. In young mutton, the fat readily separates; in old, it is held together by strings of skin. In sheep diseased of the rot, the flesh is very pale-coloured, the fat inclining to yellow, the meat appears loose from the bone, and, if squeezed, drops of water ooze out from the grains; after cooking, the meat drops clean away from the bones. Wether mutton is preferred to that of the ewe; it may be known by the lump of fat on the inside of the thigh.

PORK – When good, the rind is thin, smooth, and cool to the touch; when changing, from being too long killed, it becomes flaccid and clammy. Enlarged glands, called kernels, in the fat, are marks of an ill-fed or diseased pig.

LAMB – This meat will not keep long after it is killed. The large vein in the neck is bluish in colour when the fore quarter is fresh, green when becoming stale. In the hind quarter, if not recently killed, the fat of the kidney will have a slight smell, and the knuckle will have lost its firmness.

BACON should have a thin rind, and the fat should be firm and tinged red by the curing; the flesh should be of a clear red, without intermixture of yellow, and it should firmly adhere to the bone. To judge the state of a ham, plunge a knife into it to the bone; on drawing it back, if particles of meat adhere to it, or if the smell is disagreeable, the curing has not been effectual, and the ham is not good; it should, in such a state, be immediately cooked. In buying a ham, a short thick one is to be preferred to one long and thin. Of English hams, Yorkshire, Westmoreland, and Hampshire, are most esteemed; of foreign, the Westphalia.

VENISON – When good, the fat is clear, bright, and of considerable thickness. To know when it is necessary to cook it, a knife must be plunged into the haunch; and from the smell the cook must determine on dressing or keeping it.

TURKEY – In choosing poultry, the age of the bird is the chief point to be attended to. An old turkey has rough and reddish legs; a young one smooth and black. Fresh killed, the eyes are full and clear, and the feet moist. When it has been kept too long, the parts about the vent begin to wear a greenish discoloured appearance.

COMMON DOMESTIC FOWLS, when young, have the legs and combs smooth; when old they are rough, and on the breast long hairs are found instead of feathers. Fowls and chickens should be plump on the breast, fat on the back, and white-legged.

GEESE – The bills and feet are red when old, yellow when young. Fresh killed, the feet are pliable, stiff when too long kept. Geese are called green while they are only two or three months old.

DUCKS – Choose them with supple feet and hard plump breasts. Tame ducks have yellow feet, wild ones red.

PIGEONS are very indifferent food when they are too long kept. Suppleness of the feet show them to be young; the state of the flesh is flaccid when they are getting bad from keeping. Tame pigeons are larger than the wild.

HARES AND RABBITS, when old, have the haunches thick, the ears dry and tough, and the claws blunt and ragged. A young hare has claws smooth and sharp, ears that easily tear, and a narrow cleft in the lip. A leveret is distinguished from the hare by a knob or small bone near the foot.

PARTRIDGES, when young, have yellow legs and dark-coloured bills. Old partridges are very indifferent eating.

WOODCOCKS AND SNIPES, when old, have the feet thick and hard; when these are soft and tender, they are both young and fresh killed. When their bills become moist, and their throats muddy, they have been too long killed.

THE ENGLISH, generally speaking, are very deficient in the practice of culinary economy; a French family would live well on what is often wasted in an English kitchen: the bones, drippings, pot-liquor, remains of fish, vegetables, &c., which are too often consigned to the grease-pot or the dust-heap, might, by a very trifling degree of management on the part of the cook, or mistress of a family, be concerted into sources of daily support and comfort.

DR. KITCHENER'S RULES FOR MARKETING – The best rule for marketing is to pay ready money for every thing, *and to deal with the most respectable tradesman* in your neighbourhood. If you leave it to their integrity to supply you with a good article, at the fair market price, you will be supplied with better provisions, and at as reasonable a rate as those *bargain-hunters*, who trot "*around, around, around about*" a market till they are trapped to buy some *unchewable* old poultry, *tough* tup-mutton, *stringy* cow-beef, or *stale* fish, at a very little less than the price of prime and proper food. With *savings* like these they toddle home in triumph, cackling all the way, like a goose that has got ankle-keep in good-luck. All the skill of the most accomplished cook will avail nothing unless she is furnished with prime provisions. The best way to procure these is to deal with shops of established character – you may appear to pay, perhaps, ten *per cent.* more than you would were you to deal with those who pretend to sell cheap, but you would be much more than in that proportion better served. Every trade has its tricks and deceptions; those who follow them can deceive you if they please, and they are too apt to do so, if you provoke the exercise of their over-reaching talent. Challenge them to a game at "*Catch who can*," by entirely relying on your own judgment, and you will soon find nothing but very long experience can make you equal to the combat of marketing to the utmost advantage. If you think a tradesman has imposed upon you, never use a second word, if the first will not do, nor drop the least hint of an imposition; the only method to induce him to make an abatement is the hope of future favours, pay the demand, and deal with the gentleman no more; but do not let him see that you are displeased, or as soon as you are out of sight your reputation will suffer as much as your pocket has. Before you go to market, look over your larder, and consider well what things are

wanting – especially on a Saturday. No well-regulated family can suffer a disorderly caterer to be jumping in and out to make purchases on a Sunday morning. You will be enabled to manage much better if you will make out a bill of fare for the week on the Saturday before; for example, for a family of half a dozen –

Sunday – Roast beef and pudding.

Monday – Fowl, what was left of pudding fried, or warmed in the Dutch oven.

Tuesday – Calf's head, apple pie.

Wednesday – Leg of mutton.

Thursday – Ditto broiled or hashed, and pancakes.

Friday – Fish, pudding.

Saturday – Fish, or eggs and bacon.

It is an excellent plan to have certain things on certain days. When your butcher and poulterer knows what you will want, he has a better chance of doing his best for you; and never think of ordering beef for roasting except for Sunday. When you order meat, poultry, or fish, tell the tradesman when you intend to dress it: he will then have it in his power to serve you with provision that will do him credit, which the finest meat, &c., in the world will never do, unless it has been kept a proper time to be ripe and tender. – *Cook's Oracle.*

NAMES AND SITUATIONS OF THE JOINTS – In different parts of the kingdom the method of cutting up carcases varies. That which we describe below is the most general, and is known as the English method.

BEEF – *Fore Quarter* – Fore rib (five ribs); middle rib (four ribs); chuck (three ribs). Shoulder piece (top of fore leg); brisket (lower or belly part of the ribs); clod (fore shoulder blade); neck; shin (below the shoulder); cheek. *Hind Quarter* – Sirloin; rump; aitch-bone – these are the three divisions of the upper part of the quarter; buttock and mouse-buttock, which divide the thigh; veiny piece, joining the buttock; thick flank and thin flank (belly pieces) and leg. The sirloin and rump of both sides form a baron. *Beef is in season all the year: best in the winter.*

MUTTON – Shoulder; breast (the belly); over which are the loin (chump, or tail end). Loin (best end); and neck (best end); neck (scrag end). A chine is two necks: a saddle two loins; then there are the leg and head. *Mutton is the best in Winter, Spring, and Autumn.*

LAMB is cut into fore quarter and hind quarter; a saddle, or loin; neck, breast, leg, and shoulder. *Grass lamb is in season from Easter to Michaelmas; house lamb from Christmas to Lady-day.*

PORK is cut into leg, hand, or shoulder; hind-loin; fore-loin; belly-part; spare-rib (or neck); and head. *Pork is in season nearly all the year.*

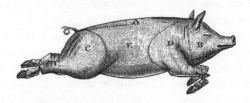

VEAL is cut into neck (scrag end); neck (best end); loin (best end); loin (chump, or tail end); fillet (upper part of hind leg); hind knuckle (which joins the fillet; knuckle of fore leg; blade (bone of shoulder); breast, (best end); breast (brisket end), and hand. *Veal is always in season, but dear in the winter and spring.*

VENISON is cut into haunch (or back); neck; shoulder; and breast. *Doe venison is best in January, October, November, and December, and buck venison in June, July, August, and September.*

ACCORDING TO THE ENGLISH METHOD the carcase of beef is disposed of more economically than upon the Scotch plan. The English plan affords better steaks, and better joints for roasting; but the Scotch plan gives a greater variety of pieces for boiling. The names of pieces in the Scotch plan, not found in the English, are the hough, or hind leg; the nincholes, or English buttock; the large and small runner, taken from the rib and chuck pieces of the English plan; the shoulder-lyer, the English shoulder, but cut differently; the spare-rib or foresye, the sticking piece, &c. The Scotch also cut the mutton differently.

OX-TAIL is much esteemed for purposes of soup; so also is the cheek. The tongue is highly esteemed.

CALVES' HEADS are very useful for various dishes; so also their knuckles, feet, heart, &c.

RELATIVE ECONOMY OF THE JOINTS

The round is, in large families, one of the most profitable parts: it is usually boiled, and, like most of the boiling parts of beef, is generally sold in London at a penny per pound less than roasting joints.

The brisket is also a penny a pound less in price than the roasting parts. It is not so economical a part as the round, having more bone to be weighed with it, and more fat. Where there are children, very fat joints are not desirable, being often disagreeable to them, and sometimes prejudicial, especially if they have a dislike to it. This joint also requires more cooking than many others; that is to say, it requires a double allowance of time to be given for boiling it; it will, when served, be hard and scarcely digestible if no more time be allowed to boil it than that which is sufficient for other joints and meats. When stewed it is excellent; and when cooked fresh (*i.e.* unsalted), an excellent stock for soup may be extracted from it, and yet the meat will serve as well for dinner.

The edgebone, or aitchbone, is not considered to be a very economical joint, the bone being large in proportion to the meat; but the greater part of it, at least, is as good as that of any prime part. It sells at a penny a pound less than roasting joints.

The rump is the part of which the London butcher makes great profit, by selling it in the form of steaks. In the country, as there is not

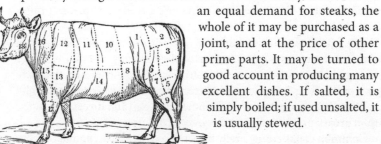

an equal demand for steaks, the whole of it may be purchased as a joint, and at the price of other prime parts. It may be turned to good account in producing many excellent dishes. If salted, it is simply boiled; if used unsalted, it is usually stewed.

The veiny piece is sold at a low price per pound; but, if hung for a day or two, it is very good and very profitable. Where there are a number of servants and children to have an early dinner, this part of beef will be found desirable.

From the leg and shin excellent stock for soup may be drawn; and, if not reduced too much, the meat taken from the bones may be served as a stew with vegetables; or it may be seasoned, pounded with butter, and potted; or chopped very fine, and seasoned with herbs, and bound together by egg and bread-crumbs; it may be fried in balls, or in the form of large eggs, and served with a gravy made with a few spoonfuls of the soup.

Of half an ox cheek excellent soup may be made; the meat, when taken from the bones, may be served as a stew.

Roasting parts of beef are the sirloin and the ribs, and these bear in all places the highest price. The most profitable of these two joints at a family table is the ribs. The bones, if removed from the beef before it is roasted, will assist in forming the basis of a soup. When boned, the meat of the ribs is often rolled up, tied with strings, and roasted; and this is the best way of using it, as it enables the carver to distribute equally the upper part of the meat with the more skinny and fatter parts at the lower end of the bones.

COOKING

Ten pounds of beef require from two hours to two hours and a half roasting, eighteen inches from a good clear fire.

Six pounds require one hour and a quarter to one hour and a half, fourteen inches from a good clear fire.

Three ribs of beef, boned and rolled, tied round with paper, will require two hours and a half, eighteen inches from the fire: baste once only.

The first three ribs, of fifteen or twenty pounds, will take three hours or three and a half; the fourth and fifth ribs will take as long, managed in the same way as the sirloin. Paper the fat and the thin part, or it will be done too much, before the thick part is done enough.

When beef is very fat, it does not require basting; if very lean tie it up in greasy paper, and baste frequently and well.

Common cooks are generally fond of too fierce a fire, and of putting things too near to it.

Slow roasting is as advantageous to the tenderness and flavour of meat as slow boiling.

The warmer the weather, and the staler killed the meat is, the less time it will require to roast it.

Meat that is very fat requires more time than other meat.

"In the hands of an expert cook," says Majendie, "alimentary substances are made almost entirely to change their nature, their form, consistence, odour, savour, colour, chemical composition, &c., everything is so modified, that it is often impossible for the most exquisite sense of taste to recognise the substance which makes up the basis of certain dishes. The greatest utility of the kitchen consists in making the food agreeable to the senses, and rendering it easy of digestion."

Boiling extracts a portion of the juice of meat, which mixes with the water, and also dissolves some of its solids; the more fusible parts of the fat melt out, combine with the water, and form soup or broth. The meat loses its red colour, becomes more savoury in taste and smell, and more firm and digestible. If the process is continued *too long*, the meat becomes indigestible, less succulent, and tough.

To boil meat to perfection, it should be done slowly, in plenty of water, replaced by other hot water as evaporation takes place; for, if boiled too quickly, the outside becomes tough; and, not allowing the ready transmission of heat, the interior remains rare.

The loss by boiling varies, according to Professor Donovan, from 6¼ to 16 per cent. The average loss on boiling butcher's meat, pork, hams, and bacon, is 12; and on domestic poultry, is 14¾.

The loss per cent. on boiling salt beef is 15; on legs of mutton, 10; hams, 12½; salt pork, 13 1/3; knuckles of veal, 8 1/3; bacon, 6¼; turkeys, 16; chickens, 13½.

The established rule as regards time, is to allow a quarter of an hour for each pound of meat if the boiling is rapid, and twenty minutes if slow. There are exceptions to this; for instance, ham and pork, which require from twenty to twenty-five minutes per pound, and bacon nearly half an hour. For solid joints allow fifteen minutes for every pound, and from ten to twenty minutes over; though, of course, the length of time will depend much on the strength of the fire, regularity in the boiling, and size of the joint. The following table will be useful as an average of the time required to boil the various articles:–

		H.	M.
A ham, 20 lbs. weight, requires		6	30
A tongue (if dry), after soaking		4	0
A tongue, out of pickle	2½ to	3	0
A neck of mutton		1	30
A chicken		0	20
A large fowl		0	45
A capon		0	35
A pigeon		0	15

Roasting, by causing the contraction of the cellular substance which contains the fat, expels more fat than boiling. The free escape of watery particles in the form of vapour, so necessary to produce flavour, must be regulated by frequent basting with the fat which has exuded from the meat, combined with a little salt and water – otherwise the meat would burn, and become hard and tasteless. A brisk fire at first will, by charring the outside, prevent the heat from penetrating, and therefore should only be employed when the meat is half roasted.

The loss of roasting varies, according to Professor Donovan, from 14 3-5ths to nearly double that rate, per cent. The average loss on roasting butcher's meat is 22 per cent.; and on domestic poultry is 20½.

The loss per cent. on roasting beef, viz., on sirloins and ribs together, is 19 1-6th; on mutton, viz., legs and shoulders together, 24 4-5ths; on fore-quarters of lamb, 22 1-3rd; on ducks, 27 1-5th; on turkeys, 20½; on geese, 19½; on chickens, 14 3-5ths. So that it will be seen by comparison with the per centage given of the loss by boiling, that roasting is not so economical; especially when we take into account that the loss of weight by boiling is not actual loss of economic materials, for we then possess the principal ingredients for soups; whereas, after roasting, the fat only remains. The average loss in boiling and roasting together is 18 per cent. according to Donovan, and 28 per cent. according to Wallace – a difference that may be

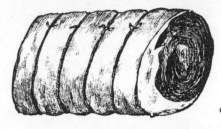

accounted for by supposing a difference in the fatness of the meat, duration and degree of heat, &c., employed.

The time required to roast various articles of food with a clear good fire, is as follows:–

		H.	M.
A small capon, fowl, or chicken, requires		0	20
A large fowl		0	45
A capon, full size		0	35
A goose		1	0
Wild ducks, and grouse		0	15
Pheasants, and Turkey poults		0	20
A moderate sized turkey, stuffed		1	15
Partridges		0	25
Quail		0	10
A hare, or rabbit	about	1	0
Beef, ten pounds		2	30
Leg of pork, ¼ hour for each pound, and above that allow		0	20
A chine of pork		2	0
A neck of mutton		1	30
A haunch of venison about		3	30

To roast properly, meat should be put a good distance from the fire, and brought gradually nearer when about half the time required for cooking it has elapsed; it should be basted frequently; and when nearly done, floured to make it look frothed. Old meats do not require so much dressing as young; and if not fat enough, use a little dripping for basting. Veal and mutton requires a little paper put over the fat, to preserve it from being burnt.

If roasting with a spit, be careful to have it well cleaned before running it through the meat, which should be done always in the inferior parts; but in many joints the spit will pass into the bones, and run along them for some distance, so as not to stain or injure the prime part. Balance skewers will frequently be required.

Broiling requires a brisk rapid heat, which, by producing a greater degree of change in the affinities of the raw meat than roasting, generates a higher flavour, so that broiled meat is more savoury than roast. The surface becoming charred, a dark-coloured crust is formed, which retards the evaporation of the juices; and, therefore, if properly done, broiled may be as tender and juicy as roasted meat.

Baking does not admit of the evaporation of the vapours so rapidly as by the processes of broiling and roasting; the fat is also retained more, and becomes converted by the agency of the heat into an empyreumatic oil, so as to render the meat less fitted for delicate stomachs, and more difficulty to digest. The meat is, in fact, partly boiled in its own confined water, and partly roasted by the dry hot air of the oven.

The loss by baking has not been estimated; and, as the time required to cook many articles must vary with their size, nature, &c., we have considered it better to leave that until giving the receipts for them.

Frying is of all methods the most objectionable, from the foods being less digestible when thus prepared, as the fat employed undergoes chemical changes. Olive oil in this respect is preferable to lard or butter. The crackling noise which accompanies the process of frying meat in a pan is occasioned by the explosions of steam formed in fat, the temperature of which is much above 212 degrees. If the meat is very juicy it will not fry well, because it becomes sodden before the water is evaporated; and it will not brown because the temperature is too low to scorch it. To fry fish well the fat should be boiling hot (600 degrees), and the fish *well dried* in a cloth, otherwise, owing to the generation of steam, the temperature will fall so low that it will be boiled in its own steam, and not be browned. Meat, or indeed any article, should be frequently turned and agitated during frying, to promote the evaporation of the watery particles. To make fried things look well, they should be done over *twice* with egg and stale bread-crumbs.

To some extent the claims of either process of cooking depends upon the taste of the individual. Some persons may esteem the peculiar flavour of fried meats, while others will prefer broils or stews. It is important, however, to understand the theory of each method of cooking, so that whichever may be adopted, it may be done well. Bad cooking, though by a good method, is far inferior to good cooking by a bad method.

CURRIED BEEF, MADRAS WAY – Take about two ounces of butter, and place it in a saucepan, with two small onions cut up into slices, and let them fry until they are a light brown; then add a table-spoonful and a half of curry powder, and mix it up well. Now put in the beef cut into pieces about an inch square; pour in from a quarter to a third of a pint of milk, and let it simmer for thirty minutes; then take it off, and place it in a dish, with a little lemon juice. Whilst cooking stir constantly, to prevent it burning. Send to table with a wall of mashed potatoes or boiled rice round it. It greatly improves any curry to add with the milk a quarter of a cocoa-nut, scraped very small, and squeezed through muslin with a little water; this softens the taste of the curry, and, indeed, no curry should be made without it.

MEAT CAKES – Take any cold meat, game, or poultry (if under-done, all the better), mince it fine, with a little fat bacon or ham, or an anchovy; season it with a little pepper and salt; mix well, and make it into small cakes three inches long, half as wide, and half an inch thick: fry these a light brown, and serve them with good gravy, or put into a mould, and boil or bake it. N.B. Bread-crumbs, hard yolks of eggs, onions, sweet herbs, savoury spices, zest, or curry-powder, or any of the forcemeats.

OYSTER PATTIES – Roll out puff paste a quarter of an inch thick, cut it into squares with a knife, sheet eight or ten patty pans, put upon each a bit of bread the size of half a walnut; roll out another layer of paste of the same thickness, cut it as above, wet the edge of the bottom paste, and put on the top, pare them round to the pan, and notch them about a dozen times with the back of the knife, rub them lightly with yolk of egg, bake them in a hot oven about a quarter of an hour: when done, take a thin slice off the top, then with a small knife, or spoon, take out the bread and the inside paste, leaving the outside quite entire; then parboil two dozen of large oysters, strain them from their liquor, wash, beard, and cut them into four, put them into a stew-pan with an ounce of butter rolled in flour, half a gill of good cream, a little grated lemon-peel, the oyster-liquor, free from sediment, reduced by boiling to one half, some cayenne pepper, salt, and a teaspoonful of lemon-juice; stir it over a fire five minutes, and fill the patties.

STEWED SALT BEEF AND PORK A LA OMAR PASHA – Put into a canteen saucepan about 2lb. of well soaked beef, cut in eight pieces; half-pound of salt pork, divided in two, and also soaked; half-pound of rice, or six tablespoonfuls; quarter-of-a-pound of onions, or four middle-sized ones, peeled and sliced; two ounces of brown sugar, or one large tablespoonful; a quarter of an ounce of pepper, and five pints of water; simmer gently for three hours, remove the fat from the top and serve. The first time I made the above was in Sir John Campbell's camp kitchen, situated on the top of his rocky cavern, facing Sebastopol, near Cathcart's-hill, and among the distinguished pupils I had upon the occasion were Colonel Wyndham, Sir John Campbell, and Dr. Hall, Inspector-General of the army in the Crimea, and other officers. This dish was much approved at dinner, and is enough for six people, and, if the receipt be closely followed, you cannot fail to have an excellent food. The London salt meat will require only a four hours' soaking, having been only lightly pickled.

CALF'S HEAD PIE – Boil the head an hour and a half, or rather more. After dining from it, cut the remaining meat off in slices. Boil the bones in a little of the liquor for three hours; then strain it off, and let it remain till next day; then take off the fat. *To make the pie* – Boil two eggs for five minutes; let them get cold, then lay them in slices at the bottom of a pie-dish, and put alternate layers of meat and jelly, with pepper and chopped lemon also alternately, till the dish is full; cover with a crust and bake it.

BLACK HOG PUDDING – Catch the blood of a hog; to each quart of blood put a large teaspoonful of salt, and stir it without ceasing until it is cold. Simmer half a pint or a pint of Emden groats in a small quantity of water till tender; there must be no gruel. The best way of doing it is in a double saucepan, so that you need not put more water than will moisten them. Chop up (for one quart of blood) one pound of the inside fat of the hog, and a quarter of a pint of bread-crumbs, a tablespoonful of sage, chopped fine, a teaspoonful of thyme, three drachms each of allspice, salt, and pepper, and a teacupful of cream. When the blood is cold, strain it through a sieve, and mix to it the fat, then the groats, and then the seasoning. When well mixed put it into the skin of the largest guts, well cleansed; tie it in lengths of about nine inches, and boil gently for twenty minutes. Take them out when they have boiled a few minutes, and prick.

DEVIL – The gizzard and rump, or legs, &c., of a dressed turkey, capon, or goose, or mutton or veal kidney, scored, peppered, salted and broiled, sent up for a relish, being made very hot, has obtained the name of a "Devil."

COSSACK'S PLUM PUDDING – Put into a basin 1lb. of flour, ¾lb. of raisins (stoned, if time be allowed), ¾lb. of the fat of salt pork (well washed, cut into small dies, or chopped), two tablespoonfuls of sugar or treacle, and half a pint of water; mix all together; put into a cloth tied tightly; boil for four hours, and serve. If time will not admit, boil only two hours, though four are preferable. How to spoil the above: – Add anything to it.

FIRST-WATCH STEW – Cut pieces of salt beef and pork into dice, put them into a stew-pan with six whole peppercorns, two blades of mace, a few cloves, a teaspoonful of celery-seeds, and a faggot of dried sweet herbs; cover with water, and stew gently for an hour, then add fragments of carrots, turnips, parsley, or any other vegetables at hand, with two sliced onions, and some vinegar to flavour; thicken with flour or rice, remove the herbs, and pour into the dish with toasted bread, or freshly baked biscuit broken small, and serve hot. When they can be procured, a few potatoes improve it very much.

OYSTER KETCHUP – Take fine fresh Milton oysters; wash them in their own liquor, skim it, pound them in a marble mortar, to a pint of oysters add a pint of sherry, boil them up, and add an ounce of salt, two drachms of pounded mace, and one of cayenne; – let it just boil up again, skim it, and rub it through a sieve; and when cold bottle it, then cork it well, and seal it down.

OX-CHEEK STEWED – Prepare the day before it is to be eaten; clean the cheek and put it into soft water, just warm; let it lie three or four hours, then put it into cold water, and let it soak all night; next day wipe it clean, put it into a stew-pan, and just cover it with water; – skim it well when it is coming to a boil, then put two whole onions, stick two or three cloves into each, three turnips quartered, a couple of carrots sliced, two bay-leaves, and twenty-four corns of allspice, a head of celery, and a bundle of sweet herbs, pepper, and salt; add cayenne and garlic, in such proportions as the palate that requires them may desire. Let it stew gently till perfectly tender, about three hours; then take out the cheek, divide it into pieces, fit to help at table; skim, and strain the gravy; melt an ounce and a half of butter in a stew pan; stir into it as much flour as it will take up; mix with it by degrees a pint and a half of the gravy; add to it a tablespoonful of mushroom or walnut ketchup, or port wine, and give it a boil. Serve up in a soup or ragoût-dish, or make it into barley broth. This is a very economical, nourishing, and savoury meal.

FORCEMEAT BALLS (for turtle, mock turtle, or made dishes) – Pound some veal in a marble mortar, rub it through a sieve with as much of the udder as you have veal, or about a third of the quantity of butter: – put some bread-crumbs into a stew-pan, moisten them with milk, add a little chopped parsley and eschalot, rub them well together in a mortar, till they form a smooth paste; put it through a sieve, and when cold, pound, and mix all together, with the yolks of three eggs boiled hard; season it with salt, pepper, and curry powder, or cayenne, add to it the yolks of two raw eggs, rub it well together, and make small balls; ten minutes before your soup is ready, put them in.

CAYENNE PEPPER – Dr. Kitchener says (in his excellent book, *The Cook's Oracle*): – We advise those who are fond of cayenne not to think it too much trouble to make it of English chillies, – there is no other way of being sure it is genuine, – and they will obtain a pepper of much finer flavour, without half the heat of the foreign. A hundred large chillies, costing only two shillings, will produce you about two ounces

of cayenne, – so it is as cheap as the commonest cayenne. Four hundred chillies, when the stems were taken off, weighed half a pound; and when dried produced a quarter of a pound of cayenne pepper. The following is the way to make it: – Take away the stalks, and put the pods into a colander; set it before the fire; they will take full twelve hours to dry; then put them into a mortar, with one-fourth their weight of salt, and pound them, and rub them till they are as *fine as possible*, and put them into a well-stopped bottle.

A NICE WAY of serving up a fowl that has been dressed. Beat the white of two eggs to a thick froth; add a small bit of butter, or some salad oil, flour, a little lukewarm water, and two tablespoonfuls of beer, beaten altogether till it is of the consistency of very thick cream. Cut up the fowl into small pieces, strew over it some chopped parsley and shalot, pepper, salt, and a little vinegar, and let it lie till dinner time; dip the fowl in the batter, and fry it in boiling lard, of a nice light brown. Veal that has been cooked may be dressed in the same way. The above is a genuine family receipt, long practised by a French servant.

WOW WOW SAUCE – Chop parsley-leaves fine; take two or three pickled cucumbers, or walnuts, and divide into small squares, and set them by ready; put into a saucepan butter as big as an egg; when it is melted, stir into it a tablespoonful of fine flour, and half a pint of the broth of the beef: add a tablespoonful of vinegar, one of mushroom catchup, or port wine, or both, and a teaspoonful of made mustard; simmer together till it is as thick as you wish, put in the parsley and pickles to get warm, and pour it over the beef, or send it up in a sauce-tureen. This is excellent for stewed or boiled beef.

SCOTCH BROSE – This favourite Scotch dish is generally made with the liquor meat has been boiled in. Put half a pint of oatmeal into a porringer with a little salt, if there be not enough in the broth, – of which add as much as will mix it to the consistence of hasty-pudding, or a little thicker, – lastly, take a little of the fat that swims on the broth, and put it on the crowdie, and eat it in the same way as hasty-pudding.

MARROW-BONES – Saw the bones even, so that they will stand steady; put a piece of paste into the ends; set them upright in a saucepan, and boil till they are done enough: – a beef marrow-bone will require from an hour and a half to two hours; serve fresh-toasted bread with them.

BAKING, BOILING, BROILING, FRYING, ROASTING, STEWING, AND SPOILING – *A Dialogue between the Dutch Oven, the Saucepan, the Spit, the Gridiron, and the Frying-pan*, with reflections thereupon, in which all housekeepers and cooks are invited to take an interest.

WE WERE ONCE STANDING by our scullery, when all of a sudden we heard a tremendous clash and jingle – the Saucepan had tumbled into the Frying-pan; the Frying-pan had shot its handle through the ribs of the Gridiron; the Gridiron had bestowed a terrible thump upon the hollow head of the Dutch-oven; and the Spit had dealt a very skilful stroke, which shook the sides of all the combatants, and made them ring out the noises by which we were startled. Musing upon this incident, we fancied that we overheard the following dialogue:–

FRYING-PAN – Hallo, Saucepan! what are you doing here, with your dropsical corporation? Quite time that you were superannuated; you are a mere meat-spoiler. You adulterate the juices of the best joint, and give to the stomach of our master little else than watery compounds to digest.

SAUCEPAN – Well! I like your conceit! You – who harden the fibre of flesh so much, that there is no telling whether a steak came from a bullock, a horse, or a bear!

– who can't fry a slice of potato, or a miserable smelt, but you must be flooded with oil or fat, to keep your spiteful nature from burning or biting the morsel our master should enjoy. Not only that – you open your mouth so wide, that the soot of the chimney drops in, and frequently spoils our master's dinner; or you throw the fat over your sides, and set the chimney in a blaze!

SPIT – Go on! go on! six one, and half-a-dozen the other!

DUTCH-OVEN – Well, Mr. Spit, you needn't try to foment the quarrel. You require more attention than any of us; for if you are not continually watched, and helped by that useful little attendant of yours they call a Jack, your lazy, lanky figure would stand still, and you would expose the most delicious joint to the ravages of the fire. In fact, you need not only a Jack to keep you going, but a cook to constantly baste the joint confided to your care, without which our master would have but a dry bone to pick. Not only so, but you thrust your spear-like length through the best meat, and make an unsightly gash in a joint which otherwise might be an ornament to the table.

SPIT – What, Dutch oven, is that you? venerable old sobersides, with a hood like a monk! Why, you are a mere dummy – as you are placed so you remain; there you stand in one place, gaping wide and catching the coals as they fall; if you were not well watched, you would burn the one half, and sodden the other, of whatever you were required to prepare. Bad luck to *your* impertinence.

GRIDIRON – Peace! peace! we all have our merits and our demerits. – At this remark of the Gridiron, there was a general shout of laughter.

SAUCEPAN – Well, I declare, I never thought that I should have *my* merits classed with those of the miserable skeleton called a Gridiron. That is a joke! A thing with six ribs and a tail to compare with so useful a member of the *cuisine* community as myself! Why you, Gridiron, waste one half of the goodness of the meat in the fire, and the other half you send to the table tainted with smoke, and burnt to cinders! – A loud rattle of approbation went round, as the poor Gridiron fell under this torrent of derision from the Saucepan.

COMING AWAY FROM THE SCENE of confusion, I ordered the scullerymaid to go instantly and place each of the utensils that lay in disorder upon the ground, into its proper place, charging her to cleanse each carefully, until it should be required for use.

THERE IS ONE PROCESS to which we must yet allude – the process of *spoiling*. Many cooks know how to *produce* a good dish, but too many of them know how to spoil it. They leave fifty things to be done just at the critical moment when the chief dish should be watched with an eye of keenness, and attended by a hand thoroughly expert. Having spent three hours in making a joint hot and rich, they forget that a quarter of an hour, after it is taken from the fire, may impair or spoil all their labours. The serving-up of a dinner may be likened to the assault upon Sebastopol. Looking upon the joint as the Malakhoff, and the surrounding dishes as the redans, the bastions, and the forts, they should all be seized simultaneously, and made the prize of the commander-in-chief, and his staff around the dinner-table. Such a victory will always do the cook the highest honour, and entitle him to the gratitude of the household.

WHY DOES A POLISHED metal teapot make better tea than a black earthen one? – As polished metal is a very bad radiator of heat, it keeps the water hot much longer; and the hotter the water is, the better it "draws" the tea.

WHY WILL NOT A DULL black teapot make good tea?
– Because the heat of the water flies off so quickly, through the dull black surface of the teapot, that the water is very rapidly cooled, and cannot "draw" the tea.

DO NOT PENSIONERS, and aged cottagers, generally prefer the black earthen teapot to the bright metal one? – Yes, because they set it on the hob to "draw;" in which case, the little black teapot will make the best tea.

WHY WILL A BLACK TEAPOT make better tea than a bright metal one, if it is set upon the hob to draw? – Because the black teapot will absorb heat plentifully from the fire, and keeps the water hot; whereas a bright metal teapot (set upon the hob) would throw off the heat by reflection.

THEN SOMETIMES A BLACK earthen teapot is the best, and sometimes a bright metal one? – Yes; when the teapot is set on the hob to "draw," the black earth is the best, because it absorbs heat; but when the teapot is not set on the hob, the bright metal is the best, because it radiates heat very slowly, and therefore keeps the water hot.

WHY DOES A SAUCEPAN which has been used boil in a shorter time than a new one? – Because the bottom and back are covered with soot, and the black soot rapidly absorbs the heat of the glowing coals.

WHY SHOULD THE FRONT and lid of a saucepan be clean and bright? – As they do not come in contact with the fire, they cannot absorb heat, and (being bright) they will not suffer the heat to escape by radiation.

WHY SHOULD NOT THE BOTTOM and back of a kettle be cleaned and polished? – Because they come in contact with the fire, and (while they are covered with black soot) absorb heat freely from the burning coals.

WHY ARE DINNER COVERS MADE OF bright tin or silver? – Because light-coloured and highly-polished metal is a very bad radiator of heat; and, therefore, bright tin or silver will not allow the heat of the cooked food to escape through the cover by radiation.

WHY SHOULD A MEAT-COVER be very brightly polished? – If the cover be dulled or scratched, it will absorb heat from the food; and instead of keeping it hot, will make it cold.

WHY SHOULD A SILVER MEAT-COVER be plain, and not chased? – Because, if the cover be chased, it will absorb heat from the food; and instead of making it hot, will make it cold.

MISS ACTON'S OBSERVATIONS ON OMELETTES, PANCAKES, FRITTERS, &C. – There is no difficulty in making good omelettes, pancakes, or fritters; and, as they may be expeditiously prepared and served, they are often a very convenient resource when, on short notice, an addition is required to a dinner. The eggs for all of them should be well and lightly whisked; the lard for frying batter should be extremely pure in flavour, and quite hot when the fritters are dropped in; the batter itself should be smooth as cream, and it should be briskly beaten the instant before it is used. All fried pastes should be perfectly drained from the fat before they are served, and sent to table promptly when they are ready. Eggs may be dressed in a multiplicity of ways, but are seldom more relished in any form than in a well-made and expeditiously-served omelette. This may be plain, or seasoned with minced herbs and a very little eschalot, when the last is liked, and is then called *Omelettes aux fines herbes*; or it may be mixed with minced ham or grated cheese; in any case, it should be light, thick, full-tasted, and *fried only on one side*; if turned in the pan, as it frequently is in England, it will at once be flattened and rendered tough. Should the slight rawness which is sometimes found in the middle of the inside, when the omelette is made in the French way, be objected to, a heated shovel, or a salamander, may be held over it for an instant, before it is folded on the dish. The pan for frying it should be quite small; for if it be composed of four or five eggs only, and then put into a large one, it will necessarily spread over it and be thin, which would render it more like a pancake than an omelette; the only partial remedy for this, when a pan of proper size cannot be had, is to raise the handle of it high, and to keep the opposite side close down to the fire, which will confine the eggs into a smaller space. No gravy should be poured into the dish with it, and indeed, if properly made, it will require none. Lard is preferable to butter for frying batter, as it renders it lighter; but it must not be used for omelettes.

BAD BUTTER may be improved greatly by dissolving it thoroughly in hot water; let it cool, then skim it off, and churn again, adding a little good salt and sugar. A small quantity can be tried and approved before doing a larger one. The water should be merely hot enough to melt the butter, or it will become oily.

SALT BUTTER may be freshened by churning it with new milk in the proportion of a pound of butter to a quart of milk. Treat the butter in all respects in churning as fresh. Cheap earthenware churns for domestic use may be had at any hardware shop.

PURE AND CHEAP BREAD – Our informant states that for more than twelve months he has ground his own flour by a small hand-mill, which produces 17lb. of good meal bread for 20lb. of wheat (quite good enough for any one to eat), and that since himself and family have used this bread they have never had occasion for medical advice. They also use the same meal for puddings, &c. The price of a mill is £4.10s. There are mills which grind and dress the wheat at one operation. To grind 20lbs. of wheat would take a boy, or a servant, about forty or fifty minutes. Such mills can be obtained at the agricultural machinery department of the Crystal Palace, or at 266, High Holborn. The saving in the cost of bread amounts to nearly one-third, which would soon cover the cost of the mill, and effect a most important saving, besides promoting health, by avoiding the evil effects of adulterated flour.

CALVES' FEET JELLY – It is better to buy the feet from the butcher, than at the tripe-shop ready boiled, because the best portion of the jelly has been extracted. Slit them in two, and take every particle of fat from the claws; wash well in warm water, put them in a large stew-pan, and cover with water; skim well and let boil gently six or seven hours, until reduced to about two quarts, then strain and skim off any oily substance on the surface. It is best to boil the feet the day before making the jelly, as, when the liquor is cold, the oily part being at the top, and the other being firm, with pieces of kitchen paper applied to it, you may remove every particle of the oily substance without wasting the liquor. Put the liquor in a stew-pan to melt, with a pound of lump sugar, the peel of two, and the juice of six lemons, six whites and shells of eggs beat together, and a bottle of sherry or Madeira; whisk the whole together until it is on the boil, then put it by the side of the stove, and let it simmer a quarter of an hour; strain it through a jelly-bag; what is strained first must be poured into the bag again, until it is as bright and clear as rock water; then put the jelly in moulds, to be cold and firm; if the weather is too warm, it requires some ice. When it is wished to be very *stiff*, half an ounce of isinglass may be added when the wine is put in. It may be flavoured by the juices of various fruits and spices, &c., and coloured with saffron, cochineal, red beet-juice, spinach-juice, claret, &c., and it is sometimes made with cherry brandy, red noyeau, curaçoa, or essence of punch.

ECONOMICAL FAMILY PUDDING – Bruise with a wooden spoon, through a colander, six large or twelve middle-sized boiled potatoes; beat four eggs, mix with a pint of good milk, stir in the potatoes; sugar and seasoning to taste; butter a dish; bake half an hour. This receipt is simple and economical, as it is made of what is wasted in most families, viz. – cold potatoes, which may be kept two or three days, till a sufficient quantity is collected. It is a weekly dish at our table. A teaspoonful of Scotch chip marmalade makes a delicious seasoning.

PARSNIP WINE – Take fifteen pounds of sliced parsnips, and boil until quite soft in five gallons of water; squeeze the liquor well out of them, run it through a sieve, and add three pounds of coarse lump sugar to every gallon of liquor. Boil the whole for three quarters of an hour. When it is nearly cold, add a little yeast on toast. Let it remain in a tub for ten days, stirring it from the bottom every day; then put it into a cask for a year. As it works over, fill it up every day.

TURNIP WINE – Take a large number of turnips, pare and slice them; then place in a cider-press, and obtain all the juice you can. To every gallon of juice add three pounds of lump sugar, and half a pint of brandy. Pour into a cask, but do not bung until it has done working; then bung it close for three months, and draw off into another cask; when it is fine, bottle, and cork well.

ELEGANT BREAD PUDDING – Take light white bread, and cut in thin slices. Put into a pudding-shape a layer of any sort of preserve, then a slice of bread, and repeat until the mould is almost full. Pour over all a pint of warm milk, in which four beaten eggs have been mixed; cover the mould with a piece of linen, place it in a saucepan with a little boiling water, let it boil twenty minutes, and serve with pudding sauce.

MOTHER EVE'S PUDDING

If you would have a good pudding, observe what
    you're taught:—
Take two pennyworth of eggs, when twelve for the
    groat;
And of the same fruit that Eve had once chosen,
Well pared and well chopp'd, at least half-a-dozen;
Six ounces of bread, (let your maid eat the crust,)
The crumbs must be grated as small as the dust;
Six ounces of currants from the stones you must
    sort,
Lest they break out your teeth, and spoil all your
    sport;
Five ounces of sugar won't make it too sweet;
Some salt and some nutmeg will make it
    complete,
Three hours let it boil, without hurry or flutter,
And then serve it up, without sugar or butter.

Entertaining & Etiquette

CEREMONIES OF THE TABLE, &C. – A dinner-table should be well laid, well lighted, and always afford a little spare room. It is better to invite one friend less in number, than to destroy the comfort of the whole party.

THE LAYING OUT OF A TABLE must greatly depend upon the nature of the dinner or supper, the taste of the host, the description of the company, and the appliances possessed. It will be useless, therefore, to lay down specific rules. The whiteness of the table-cloth, the clearness of glass, the polish of plate, and the judicious distribution of ornamental groups of fruits and flowers, are matters deserving the utmost attention.

A CROWDED TABLE MAY BE GREATLY relieved by a side-board close at hand, upon which may be placed many things incidental to the successive courses, until they are required.

AT LARGE DINNER PARTIES, where there are several courses, it is well to have the Bill of Fare neatly inscribed upon small tablets, and distributed about the table, that the diners may know what there is to come.

NAPKINS should be folded neatly. The French method, which is very easy, of folding the napkin like a fan, placing it in a glass, and spreading out the upper part, is very pleasing. But the English method of folding it like a slider, and placing the bread inside of it, is convenient as well as neat.

BREAD should be cut into thick squares, the last thing after the table is laid. If cut too early it becomes dry. A tray should be provided in which there should be a further supply of bread, new, stale, and brown. For cheese pulled bread should be provided.

CARVING-KNIVES should "be put in edge" before the dinner commences, for nothing irritates a good carver, or perplexes a bad one, more than a knife which refuses to perform its office; and there is nothing more annoying to the company than to see the carving-knife dancing to and fro over the steel, while the dinner is getting cold, and their appetites are being exhausted by delay.

JOINTS THAT REQUIRE CARVING should be set upon dishes sufficiently large. The space of the table may be economised by setting upon small dishes those things that do not require carving.

HOWEVER CLOSELY THE DINERS are compelled to sit together, *the carver should have plenty of room.*

IF THE TABLE IS VERY CROWDED, the vegetables may be placed upon the sideboard, and handed round by the waiters.

IT WOULD SAVE A GOOD DEAL OF TIME, and much disappointment, if geese, turkeys, poultry, sucking-pigs, &c., were *carved before being sent to table*; especially in those cases where the whole or the principal part of such dishes are likely to be consumed.

IT IS BEST FOR THE CARVER to supply the plates, and let the waiter hand them round, instead of putting the question to each guest as to which part he prefers, and then striving to serve him with it, to the prejudice of others present.

LADIES should be assisted before gentlemen.

WAITERS should present dishes on the left hand; so that the diner may assist himself with his right.

WINE should be taken after the first course; and it will be found more convenient to let the waiter serve it, than to hand the decanters round, or to allow the guests to fill for themselves.

WAITERS should be instructed to remove whatever articles upon the table are thrown into disuse by the progress of the dinner, as soon as they are at liberty.

FINGER-GLASSES, or glass or plated bowls, filled with rose or orange water, slightly warm in winter, or iced in summer, should be handed round.

WHEN THE DESSERT IS SERVED, the wine should be set upon the table, and the decanters passed round by the company.

FRIED FISH should be divided into suitable slices, before the fire, as soon as it leaves the frying-pan.

COD'S HEAD AND SHOULDERS – The thick part of the back is best. It should be carved in unbroken slices, and each solid slice should be accompanied by a bit of the sound from under the back-bone, or from the cheek, jaws, tongue, &c., of the head.

TURBOT – Strike the carver along the back-bone which runs from head to tail, and then serve square slices from the thick part, accompanying each slice with some of the gelatinous skin of the fins and thin part, which may be raised by laying the fish-slice flat.

JOHN DORY is served in the same way. The latter has a favourite piece on the cheek.

PLAICE, AND FLAT-FISH generally, are served in the same manner.

SOLES, when large, may be served as turbot; but when small, should be sliced across.

SALMON – Serve a slice of the thick with a smaller slice of the thin part. Keep the flakes of the thick part as firm as possible.

MACKEREL should be served in pieces cut through the side when they are large. If small, they may be divided through the back-bone, and served in halves. The shoulder part is considered the best.

WHITING are usually fried and curled. They should be cut in half down the back, and served. The shoulder-part is best.

EELS are usually cut in slices, either for stewing or frying. The thick parts are considered best.

REMARKS – The *roes* of mackerel, the *sound* of cod, the *head* of carp, the *cheek* of John Dory, the *liver* of cod, &c., are severally considered delicacies, though not by all persons. Trout, perch, jack, hake, haddock, gurnet, &c., are all served in a similar manner.

SADDLE OF MUTTON – Cut thin slices parallel with the back-bone; or slice it obliquely from the bone to the edge.

SADDLES OF PORK OR LAMB are carved in the same manner.

HAUNCH OF MUTTON OR VENISON – Make an incision right across the knuckle-end, right into the bone, and set free the gravy. Then cut thin slices the whole length of the haunch. Serve pieces of fat with slices of lean.

RUMP OR SIRLOIN OF BEEF – The undercut, called "the fillet," is exceedingly tender, and it is usual to turn the joint and serve the fillet first, reserving the meat on the upper part to serve cold. From the upper part the slices may be cut either lengthways or crossways, at option.

RIBS OF BEEF are carved in the same way as the sirloin; but there is no fillet.

ROUND OF BEEF – First cut away the irregular outside pieces, to obtain a good surface, and then serve thin and broad slices. Serve bits of the udder fat with the lean.

BRISKET OF BEEF – Cut off the outside, and then serve long slices, cut the whole length of the bones.

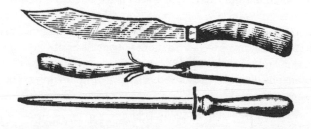

SHOULDER OF MUTTON – Make a cross incision on the fore-part of the shoulder, and serve slices from both sides of the incision; then cut slices lengthways along the shoulder-blade. Cut fat slices from the round corner.

LEG OF MUTTON – Make an incision across the centre, and serve from the knuckle-side, or the opposite, according to choice. The knuckle-side will be generally found well done, and the opposite side under-done, for those who prefer it.

LOIN OF MUTTON – Cut down between the bones, into chops.

QUARTER OF LAMB – Lay the knife flat, and cut off the shoulder. The proper point for incision will be indicated by the position of the shoulder. A little lemon-juice may be squeezed over the divided part, and a little cayenne pepper, and the shoulder transferred to another dish, for the opposite end of the table. Next separate the brisket, or short bones, by cutting lengthways along the breast. Then serve from either part as desired.

LOIN OF VEAL may be cut across through the thick part; or slices may be taken in the direction of the bones. Serve pieces of kidney and fat with each plate.

FILLET OF VEAL is carved as a round of beef. The browned bits of the outside are esteemed, and should be shared among the company, with bits of fat and of forcemeat from the centre.

BREAST OF VEAL should be divided by cutting the brisket, or soft bones, the same as the brisket of lamb. When the sweetbread comes to table with the breast, a small piece should be served on each plate.

SUCKING-PIG should be sent to table in two halves, the head divided, and one half laid at each end of the dish. The shoulders and legs should be taken off by the obvious method of laying the knife under them, and lifting the joint out. They may be served whole, or divided. The ribs are easily divided, and are considered choice.

TONGUES are cut across, in thin slices.

CALVES' HEADS are carved across the cheek, and pieces taken from any part that is come-at-able. The tongue and brain-sauce are served separate.

KNUCKLE OF VEAL is carved by cutting off the outside pieces, and then obtaining good slices, and apportioning the fat to the lean, adding bits of the sinew that lie around the joint.

LEG OF PORK is carved as a ham, but in thicker slices; when stuffed, the stuffing must be sought for under the skin at the large end.

LOIN OF PORK is carved the same as a loin of mutton.

SPARE-RIB OF PORK is carved by separating the chops, which should previously have been jointed. Cut as far as the joint, then return the knife to the point of the bones, and press over, to disclose the joint, which may then be relieved with the point of the knife.

HAMS are cut in very thin slices from the knuckle to the blade.

PHEASANTS – Carve the breast in slices. Then take off the legs and wings as a fowl.

FOWLS – Fix the fork firmly into the breast, then slip the knife under the legs, and lay it over and disjoint; then the wings in the same manner. Do the same on both sides. The smaller bones require a little practice, and it would be well to watch the operations of a good carver. When the merry-thought has been removed, which it may be by slipping the knife through at the point of the breast, and the neck-bones drawn out, the trunk may be turned over, and the knife thrust through the back bone.

PARTRIDGES are best carved by cutting off the breast, and then dividing it. But for more economical carving, the wings may be cut with a small breast slice attached.

WOODCOCKS may be cut right through the centre, from head to tail. Serve with it a piece of the toast upon which it comes to table.

PIGEONS may be carved as woodcocks, or as partridges.

SNIPES are carved the same as woodcocks.

TURKEY – Cut slices each side of the breast down to the ribs; the legs may then be removed, and the thighs divided from the drum-sticks, which are very tough; but the pinions of the wing are very good, and the white part of the wing is preferred by many to the breast.

The stuffing is usually put in the breast; but when truffles, mushrooms, or oysters are put into the body, an opening must be made into it by cutting through the apron.

GOOSE – The apron must be cut off in a circular direction, when a glass of port wine, mixed with a teaspoonful of mustard, may be poured into the body or not. Some of the stuffing should then be drawn out, and the neck of the goose being turned a little towards the carver, the flesh of the breast should be sliced on either side of the bone. The wings may then be taken off, then the legs. The other parts are carved the same as a fowl.

DUCKS may be carved, when large, the same as geese; but when young, like chickens.

THE FAMILY CIRCLE – Under this title, a series of friendly parties have been instituted by a group of acquaintances in London. The following form of invitation and the rules of the Family Circle will be found interesting, probably useful:—

Will you do me the favour of meeting here, as a guest, on — next, at seven precisely, a few friends who have kindly joined in an attempt to commence occasional, pleasant, and social parties, of which the spirit and intent will be better understood by the perusal of the few annexed remarks and rules from
Yours sincerely, —

They manage it better in France, is a remark to be often applied with reference to social life in England, and the writer fancies that the prevalence here of a few bad customs, easily changed, causes the disadvantageous difference between ourselves and our more courteous and agreeable neighbours.

1st. Worldly appearance; the phantom leading many to suppose that wealth is the standard of worth – in the minds of friends, a notion equally degrading to both parties.

2nd. Overdress; causing unnecessary expense and waste of time.

3rd. Expensive entertainments, as regards refreshments.

4th. Late hours.

The following brief rules are suggested, in a hope to show the way to a more, constant easy, and friendly inter-course amongst friends, the writer feeling convinced that society is equally beneficial and requisite – in fact, that mankind in seclusion, like the sword in the scabbard, often loses polish, and gradually rusts.

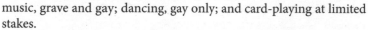

RULE 1. That meetings be held in rotation, at each member's house, for the enjoyment of conversation; music, grave and gay; dancing, gay only; and card-playing at limited stakes.

RULE 2. That such meetings commence at seven and end about or after twelve, and that members and guests be requested to remember that punctuality has been called the politeness of kings.

RULE 3. That as gentlemen are allowed for the whole season to appear, like the raven, in one suit, ladies are to have the like privilege; and that no lady be allowed to quiz or notice the habits of another lady; and that demi-toilette in dress be considered the better taste in the family circle: not that the writer wishes to raise or lower the proper standard of ladies' dress, which ought to be neither too high nor too low, but at a happy medium.

RULE 4. That any lady infringing the last rule be liable to reproof by the oldest lady present at the meeting, if the oldest lady, like the oldest inhabitant, can be discovered.

RULE 5. That every member or guest be requested to bring with them their own vocal, instrumental, or dance music, and take it away with them, if possible, to avoid loss and confusion.

RULE 6. That no member or guest able to sing, play, or dance, refuse, unless excused by medical certificate; and that no cold or sore throat be allowed to last more than a week.

RULE 7. That as every member or guest known to be able to sing, play, or dance, is bound to do so if requested, the performer (especially if timid) is to be kindly criticised and encouraged; it being a fact well known that the greatest masters of an art are always the most lenient critics, from their deep knowledge of the feeling, intelligence, and perseverance required to at all approach perfection.

RULE 8. That gentlemen present do pay every attention to ladies, especially visitors; but such attention is to be general, and not particular – for instance, no gentleman is to dance more than three times with one lady during the evening, except in the case of lovers, privileged to do odd things during their temporary lunacy, and also married couples, who are expected to dance together at least once during the evening, and oftener if they please.

RULE 9. That, to avoid unnecessary expense, the refreshments be limited to cold meat, sandwiches, bread, cheese, butter, vegetables, fruits, tea, coffee, negus, punch, malt liquors, &c. &c.

RULE 10. That all personal or face-to-face laudatory speeches (commonly called toasts, or, as may be, roasts) be for the future forbidden, without permission or enquiry, for reasons following: – That as the family circle includes bachelors and spinsters, and he, she, or they may be secretly engaged, it will be therefore cruel to excite hopes that may be disappointed; and that as some well-informed Benedict of long experience may after supper advise the bachelor to find the way to woman's heart – *vice versa*, some deep-feeling wife or widow, by "pity moven," may perhaps after supper advise the spinster the other way, which in public is an impropriety manifestly to be avoided.

RULE 11 (*suggested by a lady*). That any lady, after supper, may (if she please) ask any gentleman apparently diffident, or requiring encouragement, to dance with her, and that no gentleman can of course refuse so kind a request.

RULE 12. That no gentleman be expected to escort any lady home on foot beyond a distance of three miles, unless the gentleman be positive and the lady agreeable.

RULE THE LAST. That as the foregoing remarks and rules are intended, in perfect good faith and spirit, to be considered general and not personal, no umbrage is to be taken, and the reader is to bear in mind the common and homely saying –

"Always at trifles scorn to take offence,
It shows great pride and very little sense."

P.S. – To save trouble to both parties, this invitation be deemed accepted, without the necessity to reply, unless refused within twenty-four hours.

AN INVITATION TO A BALL should be given *at least* a week beforehand.

UPON ENTERING, FIRST ADDRESS the lady of the house; and after her, the nearest acquaintance you may recognise in the house.

IF YOU INTRODUCE A FRIEND, make him acquainted with the names of the chief persons present. But first present him to the lady of the house, and to the host.

APPEAR in full dress.

ALWAYS wear gloves.

DO NOT WEAR RINGS on the outside of your gloves.

AVOID AN EXCESS of jewellery.

DO NOT SELECT the same partner frequently.

DISTRIBUTE your attentions as much as possible.

PAY RESPECTFUL attention to elderly persons.

BE CORDIAL WHEN SERVING REFRESHMENTS, but not importunate.

IF THERE ARE MORE DANCERS than the room will accommodate, do not join in every dance.

IN LEAVING A LARGE PARTY it is unnecessary to bid farewell, and improper to do so before the guests.

A PARIS CARD OF INVITATION to an evening party usually implies that you are invited for the season.

IN BALLS AND LARGE PARTIES there should be a table for cards, and two packs of cards placed upon each table.

CHESS AND ALL UNSOCIABLE GAMES should be avoided.

ALTHOUGH MANY PERSONS do not like to play at cards except for a stake, the stakes agreed to at parties should be very trifling, so as not to create excitement or discussion.

THE HOST AND HOSTESS should look after their guests, and not confine their attentions. They should, in fact, assist those chiefly who are the least known in the room.

AVOID POLITICAL AND RELIGIOUS discussions. If you have a "hobby", keep it to yourself.

AFTER DANCING, conduct your partner to a seat.

RESIGN HER AS SOON as her next partner advances.

TERMS USED TO DESCRIBE THE MOVEMENTS OF DANCES

Balancez: Set to partners.

Chaine Anglaise: The top and bottom couples right and left.

Chaine Anglaise double: The right and left double.

Chaine des dames: The ladies chain.

Chaine des dames double: The ladies' chain double, which is performed by all the ladies commencing at the same time.

Chassez: Move to the right and left.

Chassez croisez: Gentlemen change places with partners, and back again.

Demie Chaine Anglaise: The four opposite persons half right and left.

Demie Promenade: All eight half promenade.

Dos-à-dos: The two opposite persons pass round each other.

Demi Moulinet: The ladies all advance to the centre, giving hands, and return to places.

La grand chaine: All eight chassez quite round, giving alternately right and left hands to partners, beginning with the right.

Le grand rond: All join hands and advance and retire twice.

Pas d'Allemande: The gentlemen turn the partners under their arms.

Traversez: The two opposite persons change places.

Vis-à-vis: The opposite partner.

EVENING PASTIMES – Among the innocent recreations of the fireside, there are few more commendable and practicable than those afforded by what are severally termed Anagrams, Charades, Conundrums, Enigmas, Puzzles, Rebuses, Riddles, Transpositions, &c. Of these there are such a variety, that they are suited to every capacity; and they present this additional attraction, that ingenuity may be exercised in the *invention* of them, as well as in their solution. Many persons who have become noted for their literary compositions may date the origin of their success to the time when they attempted the composition of a trifling enigma or charade.

ANAGRAMS ARE FORMED by the transpositions of the letters of words or sentences, or names of persons, so as to produce a word, sentence, or verse of pertinent, or of widely different meaning. They are very difficult to discover, but are exceedingly striking when good. The following are some of the most remarkable:–

Transposed–	*forms–*
Astronomers	No more stars.
Catalogues	Got as a clue.
Elegant	Neat leg.
Impatient	Tim in a pet.
Immediately	I met my Delia.
Masquerade	Queen as mad.
Matrimony	Into my arm.

Melodrama...........................	Made moral.
Midshipman	Mind his map.
Old England........................	Golden land.
Parishioners	I hire parsons.
Parliament...........................	Partial men.
Penitentiary..........................	Nay I repent.
Presbyterians	Best in prayer.
Radical Reform....................	Rare mad frolic.
Revolution...........................	To love ruin.
Sir Robert Peel....................	Terrible poser.
Sweetheart...........................	There we sat.
Telegraphs	Great helps.

CONUNDRUMS – These are simple catches, in which the sense is playfully cheated, and are generally founded upon words capable of double meaning. The following are examples:–

Where did Charles the First's executioner dine, and what did he take?
He took a chop at the King's Head.

When is a plant to be dreaded more than a mad dog?
When it's madder.

What is Majesty stripped of its externals?
It is *a jest*. [The *m* and the *y*, externals, are taken away.]

Why is hot bread like a caterpillar?
Because it's the grub that makes the butter fly.

Why did the accession of Victoria throw a greater damp over England than the death of King William?
Because the King was missed (mist) *while the Queen was reigning* (raining).

Why should a gouty man make his will?
To have his legatees (leg at ease).

Why are bankrupts more to be pitied than idiots?
Because bankrupts are broken, while idiots are only cracked.

Why is the treadmill like a true convert?
Because its turning is the result of conviction.

When may a nobleman's property be said to be all feathers?
When his estates are all entails (hen-tails).

THE CHARADE is a poetical or other composition founded upon a word, each syllable of which constitutes a *noun*, and the whole of which word constitutes another noun of a somewhat different meaning from those supplied by its separate syllables. Words which fully answer these conditions are the best for the purposes of charades; though many other words are employed. In writing, the first syllable is termed "*My first*," the second syllable, "*My second*," and the complete word, "*My whole*." The following is an example of a Poetical Charade:–

The breath of the morning is sweet;
   The earth is bespangled with flowers;
And buds in a countless array
   Have oped at the touch of the showers.
The birds whose glad voices are ever
   A music delightful to hear,
Seem to welcome the joy of the morning
   As the hour of the bridal draws near.
What is that which now steals on *my first*
   Like a sound from the dream-land of love,
And seems wand'ring the valleys among—
   That they may the nuptials approve?
'Tis a sound which *my second* explains,
   And it comes from a sacred abode,
And it merrily trills as the villagers throng

> To greet the fair bride on her road.
> How meek is her dress, how befitting a bride
> So beautiful, spotless, and pure.

ENIGMAS ARE COMPOSITIONS of a different character, based upon *ideas* rather than upon words, and frequently constructed so as to mislead, and to surprise when the solution is made known. Enigmas may be founded upon simple catches, like Conundrums, in which form they are usually called Riddles, such as–

> "Though you set me on foot,
> I shall be on my head,"

The answer is, *A nail in a shoe.* The celebrated Enigma, by Lord Byron, is an admirable specimen of what may be rendered through the form of an Enigma. Mr. Philp, the Editor of the first six volumes of "The Family Friend," was the first person who gave *The Enigma* a really useful application, making it the medium for conveying scientific problems and facts, instead of merely simple catches. The prize Enigmas reprinted from "The Family Friend" in "The Family Pastime," Vol. I., already alluded to, were written by Mr. Philp, and are excellent examples. Such Enigmas will be frequently introduced in our *Monthly Interview*.

REBUSES ARE A CLASS OF ENIGMA generally formed by the first, sometimes the first and last, letters of words, or of transpositions of letters, or additions to words. Dr. Johnson, however, represents Rebus to be a word represented by a picture. And putting the Doctor's definition and our own explanation together, the reader may glean a good conception of the nature of the Rebus. Example:–

> The father of the Grecian Jove;
> A little boy who's blind;
> The foremost land in all the world,
> The mother of mankind;
> A poet whose love-sonnets are
> Still very much admired;–
> The *initial* letters will declare
> A blessing to the tired.

Answer – *S*aturn; *L*ove; *E*ngland; *E*ve; *P*lutarch. The initials form *sleep*.

There is an excellent little work just published entitled "Philosophy and Mirth, United by Pen and Pencil"; the novelty of which consists in this – that many of the Enigmas are accompanied by Enigmatical pictures, so that the eye is puzzled as well as the ear. The price is 1s. 6d.

PUZZLES VARY VERY MUCH. One of the simplest that we know is this:–

Take away half of *thirteen*, and let *eight* remain

Write XIII on a slate, or on a piece of paper – rub out the lower half of the figures, and VIII will remain.

What are termed "practical puzzles" are cut out of wood, cardboard, ivory, &c., and may be purchased at the toy-shops.

MY WIFE'S LITTLE TEA PARTIES

My wife is celebrated for her little tea parties; not tea parties alone – but dinner parties, pic-nic parties, music parties, supper parties, in fact, she is the life and soul of *all parties*, which is more than any leading politician of the day can boast. But her great *forte* is her little tea parties – praised and enjoyed by everybody. A constant visitor at these little parties is Mrs. Hitchings, and she remarks that she "never knew any one who understood the *h*art of bringing so many *h*elegancies together" as my wife. Nobody makes tea like her, and how she makes it she will impart at a future time. But for her little "nick-nacks," as she calls them, which give a variety and a charm to the tea table, without trenching too deeply upon our own pocket, she has been kind enough to give a few receipts upon the present occasion.

NICE PLUM CAKE – One pound of flour, quarter of a pound of butter, quarter of a pound of sugar, quarter of a pound of currants, three eggs, half a pint of milk, and a small teaspoonful of carbonate of soda. The above is excellent. The cakes are always baked in a common earthen *flower-pot saucer*, which is a very good plan.

GINGERBREAD SNAPS – One pound of flour, half a pound of treacle, half a pound of sugar, quarter of a pound of butter, half an ounce of best prepared ginger, sixteen drops of essence of lemon, potash the size of a nut dissolved in a tablespoonful of hot water. This has been used in my wife's family for thirty years.

DROP CAKE – One pint of flour, half a pound of butter, quarter of a pound of pounded lump sugar, half a nutmeg grated, a handful of currants, two eggs, and a large pinch of carbonate of soda, or volatile salts. To be baked in a slack oven for ten minutes or a quarter of an hour. The above quantity will make about thirty cakes. The cakes are excellent.

COMPOSITION – If you would write to any purpose, you must be perfectly free from without, in the first place, and yet more free from within. Give yourself the natural rein; think on no pattern, no patron, no paper, no press, no public; think on nothing, but follow your own impulses. Give yourself as you are, what you are, and how you see it. Every man sees with his own eyes, or does not see at all. This is incontrovertibly true. Bring out what you have. If you have nothing, be an honest beggar rather than a respectable thief. Great care and attention should be devoted to epistolary correspondence, as nothing exhibits want of taste and judgment so much as a slovenly letter. Since the establishment of the penny postage it is recognised as a rule that all letters should be prepaid; indeed, many persons make a point of never taking in an unpaid letter. The following hints may be worthy of attention:–

ALWAYS PUT A STAMP on your envelope at the top of the right-hand corner.

LET THE DIRECTION be written very plain; this will save the postman trouble, and facilitate business by preventing mistakes.

AT THE HEAD OF YOUR LETTER, in the right-hand corner, put your address in full, with the day of the month underneath; do not omit this, though you may be writing to your most intimate friend three or four times a day.

WHAT YOU HAVE TO SAY IN YOUR LETTER, say as plainly as possible, as if you were speaking: this is the best rule; do not revert three or four times to one circumstance, but finish up as you go on.

LET YOUR SIGNATURE be written as plain as possible, (many mistakes will be avoided, especially in writing to strangers) and without any flourishes, as they tend not to add in any way to the harmony of your letter. We have seen signatures that have been almost impossible to decipher, being a mere mass of strokes, without any form to indicate letters. This is done chiefly by the ignorant, and would lead one to suppose that they were ashamed of signing what they had written.

DO NOT CROSS YOUR LETTERS: surely paper is cheap enough now to admit of your using an extra half-sheet, in case of necessity. (This practice is chiefly prevalent amongst young ladies.)

IF YOU WRITE TO A STRANGER for information, or on your own business, fail not to send a stamped envelope with your address plainly written; this will not fail to procure you an answer.

IF YOU ARE NOT A GOOD WRITER it is advisable to use best ink, the best paper, and the best pens, as, though they may not alter the character of your handwriting, yet they will assist to make your writing look better.

THE PAPER ON which you write should be clean, and neatly folded.

THERE SHOULD NOT BE STAINS on the envelope; if otherwise, it is only an indication of your own slovenliness.

CARE must be taken in giving titled persons, to whom you write, their proper directions.

DIRECTIONS FOR ADDRESSING PERSONS OF RANK

THE ROYAL FAMILY

The Queen – Madam; Most Gracious Sovereign; May it please your Majesty.

To the Queen's Most Excellent Majesty.

The King – Sire, or Sir; Most Gracious Sovereign; May it please your Majesty.

To the King's Most Excellent Majesty.

The Sons and Daughters, Brothers and Sisters of Sovereigns – Sir, or Madame; May it please your Royal Highness.

To his Royal Highness the Prince of Wales.

To her Royal Highness the Duchess of Gloucester.

Other Branches of the Royal Family – Sir, or Madam, May it please your Highness.

To his Highness the Duke of Cambridge; or, To her Highness Princess Sophia of Gloucester.

THE NOBILITY

A Duke Or Duchess – My Lord, or My Lady, May it please your Grace.

To his Grace the Duke of —; or, To her Grace the Duchess of —.

A Marquis or Marchioness – My Lord, or My Lady, May it please your Lordship, or May it please your Ladyship.

To the Most Noble the Marquis (or Marchioness) of —.

An Earl or Countess – the same.

To the Right Honourable the Earl (or Countess) of —.

A Viscount or Viscountess – My Lord, or My Lady, May it please your Lordship; or, May it please your Ladyship.

To the Right Honourable Viscount (or Viscountess) —.

A Baron or Baroness – the same.

To the Right Honourable the Baron (or Baroness) —.

The Widow of a Nobleman is addressed in the same style, with the introduction of the word Dowager in the superscription.

To the Right Honourable the Dowager Countess —.

The Sons of Dukes and Marquises, and the eldest Sons of Earls, have, by courtesy, the titles of Lord and Right Honourable; and all the Daughters have those of Lady and Right Honourable.

The younger Sons of Earls, and the Sons and Daughters of Viscounts and Barons are styled Honourable.

OFFICIAL MEMBERS OF THE STATE

A Member of Her Majesty's Most Honourable Privy Council - Sir, or My Lord, Right Honourable Sir, or My Lord; as the case may require.

To the Right Honourable —, Her Majesty's Principal Secretary of State for Foreign Affairs.

Ambassadors and Governors under Her Majesty - Sir, or My Lord, as the case may be; May it please your Excellency.

To his Excellency the American (or Russian) or other Ambassador.

To his Excellency Marquis —, Lieutenant General, and General Governor of that part of the United Kingdom called Ireland.

Judges - My Lord, May it please your Lordship.

To the Right Honourable Sir Charles Abbott, Lord Chief Justice of England.

The Lord Mayor of London, York, or Dublin, and the Lord Provost of Edinburgh, during office - My Lord, May it please your Lordship.

To the Right Honourable —, Lord Mayor of London.

To the Right Honourable Sir —, Lord Provost of Edinburgh.

The Lord Provost of every other town in Scotland is styled Honourable.

The Mayors of all Corporations (excepting the preceding Lord Mayors), and the Sheriffs, Aldermen, and Recorder of London, are addressed Right Worshipful; and the Aldermen and Recorders of other Corporations, and the Justices of the Peace, Worshipful.

THE PARLIAMENT

House of Peers - My Lords, may it please your Lordships.

To the Right Honourable the Lords Spiritual and Temporal, in Parliament assembled.

House of Commons – May it please your Honourable House.

To the Honourable the Commons of the United Kingdom of Great Britain and Ireland.

The Speaker of ditto. – Sir, or Mr. Speaker.

To the Right Honourable —, Speaker of the House of Commons.

A Member of the House of Commons not ennobled – Sir.

To —, Esq., M.P.

THE CLERGY

An Archbishop – My Lord, May it please your Grace.

To his Grace the Archbishop of Canterbury; or, To the Most Reverend Father in God, —, Lord Archbishop of Canterbury.

A Bishop – My Lord, May it please your Lordship.

To the Right Reverend Father in God, —, Lord Bishop of Oxford.

A Dean – My Lord, May it please your Lordship.

To the Rev. Dr. —, Dean of Carlisle.

Archdeacons and Chancellors are addressed in the same manner.

The rest of the Clergy – Sir, Reverend Sir.

To the Rev. Dr. —, Glasgow.

To the Rev. —, — street, London; or, To the Rev. Mr. —, &c.

PARISIAN ETIQUETTE

A little book has been published under this title,* from which we compile the following rules of politeness and taste. In the work itself, they are given in a different form; and the subjects are somewhat amplified. Many of our readers may be visiting Paris, and to such persons the following hints will be useful:–

INTRODUCTION TO SOCIETY

Avoid all extravagance and mannerism, and be not over-timid at the outset.

Be discreet and sparing of your words.

Awkwardness is a great misfortune, but it is not an unpardonable fault.

To deserve the reputation of moving in good society, something more is requisite than the avoidance of blunt rudeness.

Strictly keep to your engagements.

Punctuality is the essence of royal politeness.

THE TOILET

Too much attention cannot be paid to the arrangements of the toilet.

A man is often judged by his appearance, and seldom incorrectly.

A neat exterior, equally free from extravagance and poverty, almost always proclaims a right-minded man.

To dress appropriately, and with good taste, is to respect yourself and others.

A black coat and trowsers are indispensable for a visit of ceremony, an entertainment, or a ball.

The white or black waistcoat is equally proper in these cases.

The hand should always be gloved.

A well-bred man always wears yellow kids in dancing. [So says our Parisian authority: we take exception, however, to the *yellow* – a tint is preferable to a decided colour!]

A person of distinction is always known by the fineness of his linen, and by the nicety of his hat, gloves, and boots. [Rather read: fine linen, and a good hat, gloves, and boots, are evidences of the highest taste in dress.]

A gentleman walking should always wear gloves, this being one of the characteristics of good breeding.

Upon public and state occasions officers should appear in uniform.

Ladies dresses should be chosen, so as to produce an agreeable harmony.

Never put on a dark-coloured bonnet with a light spring costume.

Avoid uniting colours which will suggest an epigram; such as a straw-coloured dress with a green bonnet.

The arrangement of the hair is most important.

Bands are becoming to faces of a Grecian caste.

Ringlets better suit lively and expressive heads.

Whatever be your style of face, avoid an excess of lace, and let flowers be few and choice.

In a married woman a richer style of ornament is admissible.

Costly elegance for her – for the young girl, a style of modest simplicity.

The most elegant dress loses its character if it is not worn with grace.

Young girls have often an air of constraint, and their dress seems to partake of their want of ease.

In speaking of her toilet, a woman should not convey the idea that her whole skill consists in adjusting tastefully some trifling ornaments.

A simple style of dress is an indication of modesty.

CLEANLINESS

The hands should receive special attention. They are the outward signs of general cleanliness. The same may be said of the face, the neck, the ears, and the teeth.

The cleanliness of the system generally, and of bodily apparel, pertains to Health, and will be treated of under this head.

THE HANDKERCHIEF

There is considerable art in using this accessory of dress and comfort.

Avoid extreme patterns, styles, and colours.

Never be without a handkerchief.

Hold it freely in the hand, and do not roll it into a ball. Hold it by the centre, and let the corners form a fan-like expansion.

Avoid using it too much. With some persons the habit becomes troublesome and unpleasant.

VISITS AND PRESENTATIONS

Friendly calls should be made in the forenoon, and require neatness, without costliness of dress.

Calls to give invitations to dinner-parties, or balls, should be very short, and should be paid in the afternoon.

Visits of condolence require a grave style of dress.

A formal visit should never be made before noon.

If a second visitor is announced, it will be proper for you to retire, unless you are very intimate, both with the host and the visitor announced; unless, indeed, the host expresses a wish for you to remain.

Visits after balls or parties should be made within a month.

In the latter, it is customary to enclose your card in an envelope, bearing the address outside. This may be sent by post, if you reside at a distance. But, in the neighbourhood, it is polite to send your servant, or to call. In the latter case a corner should be turned down.

Scrape your shoes, and use the mat. Never appear in a drawing-room with mud on your boots.

When a new visitor enters a drawing-room, if it be a gentleman the ladies bow slightly; if a lady, the guests rise.

Hold your hat in your hand, unless requested to place it down. Then lay it beside you.

The last arrival in a drawing-room takes a seat left vacant near the mistress of the house.

A lady is not required to rise on receiving a gentleman, nor to accompany him to the door.

When your visitor retires, ring the bell for the servant. You may then accompany your guest as far towards the door as the circumstances of your friendship seem to demand.

Request the servant, during the visit of guests, to be ready to attend to the door the moment the bell rings.

When you introduce a person pronounce the name distinctly, and say whatever you can to make the introduction agreeable. Such as "an old and valued friend," a "school-fellow of mine," "an old acquaintance of our family."

Never stare about you in a room as if you were taking stock.

The gloves should not be removed during a visit.

Be hearty in your reception of guests. And where you see much diffidence, assist the stranger to throw it off.

A lady does not put her address on her visiting card.

The Eternal Quest for Self-Betterment

EARLY RISING – The difference between rising every morning at six and at eight, in the course of forty years, amounts to 29,200 hours, or three years one hundred and twenty-one days and sixteen hours, which are equal to eight hours a day for exactly ten years. So that rising at six will be the same as if ten years of life (a weighty consideration) were added, wherein we may command eight hours every day for the cultivation of our minds and the despatch of business.

TEMPERANCE – "If," observes a writer, "men lived uniformly in a healthy climate, were possessed of strong and vigorous frames, were descended from healthy parents, were educated in a hardy and active manner, were possessed of excellent natural dispositions, were placed in comfortable situations in life, were engaged only in healthy occupations, were happily connected in marriage, and kept their passions in due subjection, there would be little occasion for medical rules." All this is every excellent and desirable; but, unfortunately for mankind, unattainable.

MAN must be something more than man, to be able to connect the different links of this harmonious chain – to consolidate this *summum bonum* of earthly felicity into one uninterrupted whole; for, independent of all regularity or irregularity of diet, passions, and other sublunary circumstances, contingencies, and connections, relative or absolute, thousands are visited by diseases and precipitated into the grave, independent of accident, to whom no particular vice could attach, and with whom the appetite never overstepped the boundaries of temperance. Do we not hear almost daily of instances of men living near to and even upwards of a century? We cannot account for this either; because of such men we know but few who have lived otherwise than the world around them; and we have known many who have lived in habitual intemperance for forty or fifty years without interruption and with little apparent inconvenience.

THE ASSERTION has been made by those who have attained a great age (Parr, and Henry Jenkins, for instance,) that they adopted no particular arts for the preservation of their health; consequently, it might be inferred that the duration of life has no dependence on manners or customs, or the qualities of particular food. This, however, is an error of no common magnitude.

PEASANTS, LABOURERS, and other hard-working people, more especially those whose occupations require them to be much in the open air, may be considered as following a regulated system of moderation; and hence the higher degree of health which prevails among them and their families. They also observe rules; and those which it is said were recommended by Old Parr are remarkable for good sense; namely, "keep your head cool by temperance, your feet warm by exercise; rise early, and go soon to bed; and if you are inclined to get fat, keep your eyes open and your mouth shut." In other words, sleep moderately, and be abstemious in diet; – excellent admonitions, more especially to those inclined to corpulency.

THE ADVANTAGES to be derived from a regular mode of living, with a view to the preservation of health and life, are nowhere better exemplified than in the precepts and practice of Plutarch, whose rules for this purpose are excellent; and by observing them himself, he maintained his bodily strength and mental faculties unimpaired to a very advanced age. Galen is a still stronger proof of the advantages of a regular plan, by means of which he reached the great age of 140 years, without having ever experienced disease. His advice to the readers of his "Treatise on Health," is as follows: – "I beseech all persons who shall read this work, not to degrade themselves to a level with the brutes, or the rabble, by gratifying their sloth, or by eating and drinking promiscuously whatever pleases their palates, or by indulging their appetites of every kind. But whether they understand physic or not, let them consult their reason, and observe what agrees, and what does not agree with them, that, like wise men, they may adhere to the use of such things as conduce to their health, and forbear everything which, by their own experience, they find to do them hurt; and let them be assured that, by a diligent observation and practice of this rule, they may enjoy a good share of health, and seldom stand in need of physic or physicians."

ARTIFICIAL MANNERS – Artificial manners, and such as spring from good taste and refinement, can never be mistaken, and differ as widely as gold and tinsel. How captivating is gentleness of manner derived from true humility, and how faint is every imitation: the one resembles a glorious rainbow, spanning a dark cloud – the other, its pale attendant, the water-gall. That suavity of manner which renders a real gentlewoman courteous to all, and careful to avoid giving offence, is often copied by those who merely subject themselves to certain rules of etiquette; but very awkward is the copy! Warm professions of regard are bestowed on those who do not expect them, and the esteem which is due to merit appears to be lavished on every one alike. And as true humility, blended with a right appreciation of self-respect, gives a pleasing cast to the countenance, so from a sincere and open disposition springs that artlessness of manner which disarms all prejudice. Feeling, on the contrary, is ridiculous when affected, and, even when real, should not be too openly manifested. Let the manners arise from the mind, and let there be no disguise for the genuine emotions of the heart.

SCANDAL – LIVE IT DOWN
Should envious tongues some malice frame,
To soil and tarnish your good name,

> Live it down!

Grow not dishearten'd; 'tis the lot
Of all men, whether good or not:

> Live it down!

Rail not in answer, but be calm;
For silence yields a rapid balm:

Live it down!

Go not among your friends and say,
Evil hath fallen on my way:

Live it down!

Far better thus yourself alone
To suffer, than with friends bemoan
The trouble that is all your own:

Live it down!

What though men *evil* call your *good!*
So Christ himself, misunderstood,
Was nail'd unto a cross of wood!
And now shall you, for lesser pain,
Your inmost soul for ever stain,
By rendering evil back again?

Live it down!

Oh! if you look to be forgiven,
Love your own foes, the bitterest even,
And love to you shall glide from heaven,
And when shall come the poison'd lie
Swift from the bow of calumny,
If you would turn it harmless by,
And make the venom'd falsehood lie,

Live it down!

FRUGALITY – The great philosopher, Dr. Franklin, inspired the mouth-piece of his own eloquence, "Poor Richard," with "many a gem of purest ray serene," encased in the homely garb of proverbial truisms. On the subject of frugality we cannot do better than take the worthy Mentor for our text, and from it address our remarks. A man may, if he knows not how to save as he

gets, "keep his nose all his life to the grindstone, and die not worth a groat at last. A fat kitchen makes a lean will," and,

"Many estates are spent in getting,
Since women for tea forsook spinning and knitting,
And men for punch forsook hewing and splitting."

IF YOU WOULD BE WEALTHY, think of saving as well as of getting. The Indies have not made Spain rich, because her out-goes are greater than her in-comes.

AWAY then with your expensive follies, and you will not then have so much cause to complain of hard times, heavy taxes, and chargeable families.

"WHAT MAINTAINS one vice would bring up two children."

YOU MAY THINK, perhaps, that a little tea, or superfluities now and then, diet a little more costly, clothes a little finer, and a little entertainment now and then, can be no great matter; but remember, "Many a little makes a mickle."

BEWARE OF LITTLE EXPENSES: "A small leak will sink a great ship," as Poor Richard says; and again, "Who dainties love, shall beggars prove;" and moreover, "Fools make feasts and wise men eat them."

HERE YOU ARE all got together to this sale of fineries and nick-nacks. You call them goods; but if you do not take care, they will prove evils to some of you. You expect they will be sold cheap, and, perhaps, they may for less than they cost; but if you have no occasion for them they must be dear to you.

REMEMBER what poor Richard says, "Buy what thou hast no need of, and ere long thou shalt sell they necessaries."

AND AGAIN, "At a great pennyworth, pause awhile." He means, perhaps, that the cheapness is apparent only, and not real; or the bargain, by straitening thee in thy business, may do thee more harm than good; for in another place he says, "Many have been ruined by buying good pennyworths."

AGAIN, "It is foolish to lay out money in the purchase of repentance;" and yet this folly is practised every day at auctions, for want of minding the almanack.

MANY, for the sake of finery on the back, have gone with a hungry stomach, and half starved their families. "Silks and satins, scarlets and velvets, put out the kitchen fire," as Poor Richard says. These are not the necessaries of life; they can scarcely be called the conveniences; and yet, only because they look pretty, how many want to have them!

BY THESE and other extravagances, the genteel are reduced to poverty, and forced to borrow of those whom they formerly despised, but who, through industry and frugality have maintained their standing; in which case it appears plainly, that, "A ploughman on his legs is higher than a gentleman on his knees," as Poor Richard says. Perhaps they had a small estate left them, which they knew not the getting of; they think "It is day, and will never be night;" that a little to be spent out of so much is not worth minding; but "Always taking out of the meal-tub, and never putting in, soon comes to the bottom," as Poor Richard says; and then "When the well is dry, they know the worth of water."

BUT THIS THEY MIGHT have known before, if they had taken his advice: "If you would know the value of money, go and try to borrow some; for he that goes a borrowing goes a sorrowing," as Poor Richard says; and, indeed, so does he that lends to such people, when he goes to get it in again. Poor Dick further advises:–
    "Fond pride of dress is sure a very curse;
    Ere fancy you consult, consult your purse."

AND AGAIN, "Pride is as loud a beggar as want, and a great deal more sauce."

WHEN YOU HAVE BOUGHT one fine thing, you must buy ten more, that your appearance may be all of a piece; but Poor Dick says, "It is easier to suppress the first desire than to satisfy all that follow it;" and it is as truly folly for the poor to ape the rich, as for the frog to swell in order to equal the ox.

"Vessels large may venture more,
But little boats should keep near shore."

IT IS, HOWEVER, a folly soon punished; for "Pride that dines on vanity, sups on contempt; pride breakfasted with plenty, dined with poverty, and supped with infamy."

AND, AFTER ALL, of what use is this pride of appearance, for which so much is risked, so much is suffered? It cannot promote health, nor ease pain; it makes no increase of merit in the person – it creates envy, it hastens misfortune.

HINTS UPON MONEY MATTERS – Have a supply of change in hand – shillings, sixpences, half-pence. This will obviate the various inconveniences of keeping people at the door, sending out at unreasonable times, and running or calling after any inmate in the house, supposed to be better provided with "the needful." The tradespeople with whom you regularly deal will always give you extra change, *when* you are making purchase or paying bills; while those to whom you apply for it, on a sudden emergency, may neither be willing nor able to do so. Some housekeepers object to this arrangement, that, "as soon as five-pound notes or sovereigns are changed, they always seem to go, without their understanding how;" but to such persons I would humbly intimate, that this is rather the fault of their *not getting understanding*, than any inevitable consequence of *getting change*. The fact is, that it is the necessity of parting with your money which obliges you to get the larger pieces changed, and not the circumstance of having smaller coin that *necessitates* your parting with your money, though it certainly facilitates your doing so, when the necessity arrives. However, as it is easier to count a few sovereigns than many shillings, and loose money is most objectionable, it is well to put up reserve change in small collective packets, and to replenish the housekeeping purse from these daily or weekly, as may be most convenient.

HABITS OF A MAN OF BUSINESS – A sacred regard to the principles of justice forms the basis of every transaction, and regulates the conduct of the upright man of business.

He is strict in keeping his engagements.

Does nothing carelessly or in a hurry.

Employs nobody to do what he can easily do himself.

Keeps everything in its proper place.

Leaves nothing undone that ought to be done, and which circumstances permit him to do.

Keeps his designs and business from the view of others.

Is prompt and decisive with his customers, and does not over-trade his capital.

Prefers short credits to long ones; and cash to credit at all times, either in buying or selling; and small profits in credit cases with little risk, to the chance of better gains with more hazard.

He is clear and explicit in all his bargains.

Leaves nothing of consequence to memory which he can and ought to commit to writing.

Keeps copies of all his important letters which he sends away, and has every letter, invoice, &c., belonging to his business, titled, classed, and put away.

Never suffers his desk to be confused by many papers lying upon it.

Is always at the head of his business, well knowing that if he leaves it, it will leave him.

Holds it as a maxim that he whose credit is suspected is not one to be trusted.

Is constantly examining his books, and sees through all his affairs as far as care and attention will enable him.

Balances regularly at stated times, and then makes out and transmits all his accounts current to his customers, both at home and abroad.

Avoids as much as possible all sorts of accommodation in money matters and lawsuits where there is the least hazard.

He is economical in his expenditure, always living within his income.

Keeps a memorandum-book in his pocket, in which he notes every particular relative to appointments, addresses, and petty cash matters.

Is cautious how he becomes security for any person; and is generous when urged by motives of humanity.

Let a man act strictly to these habits; when once begun they will be easy to continue in – ever remembering that he hath no profits by his pains whom Providence doth not prosper – and success will attend his efforts.

Take pleasure in your business, and it will become your recreation.

Hope for the best, think for the worst, and bear whatever happens.

TAKING A SHOP OR PLACE OF BUSINESS – If you are about to take a place of business, you will do well to consider the following remarks:

SMALL CAPITALISTS – Let us take the case of a person who has no intimate knowledge of any particular trade, but having a very small capital, is about to embark it in the exchange of commodities for cash, in order to obtain an honest livelihood thereby. It is clear, that unless such a person starts with proper precaution and judgment, the capital will be expended without adequate results; rent and taxes will accumulate, the stock will lie dead or become deteriorated, and loss and ruin must follow. For the least absorption acting upon a small capital will soon dry up its source; and we need not picture the trouble that will arise when the mainspring of a tradesman's success abides by him no more.

LARGER CAPITALISTS – The case of the larger capitalist can scarcely be considered an exception to the same rule. For it is probable that the larger capitalist, upon commencing a business, would sink more of his funds in a larger stock – would incur liability to a heavier rent; and the attendant taxes, the wages of assistants and servants, would be greater; and, therefore, if the return come not speedily, similar consequences must sooner or later ensue.

LOCALITIES – Large or small capitalists should, therefore, upon entering on a shop-keeping speculation, consider well the nature of the locality in which they propose to carry on trade, the number of the population, and the habits and wants of the people, and the extent to which they are already supplied with the goods which the new adventurer proposes to offer them.

NEW NEIGHBOURHOODS – There is a tendency among small capitalists to rush into new neighbourhoods, with the expectation of making an early connection. Low rents also serve as an attraction to these localities. We have found, however, in our experience, that the early suburban shops seldom succeed. They are generally entered upon at the very earliest moment that the state of the locality will permit – often before the house is finished the shop is tenanted, and goods exposed for sale – even while the streets are unpaved, and while the roads are as rough and uneven as country lanes. The consequence is that, as the few inhabitants of these localities have frequent communication with adjacent towns, they, as a matter of habit or of choice, supply their chief wants thereat; and the suburban shopkeeper depends principally for support upon the accidental forgetfulness of his neighbour, who omits to bring something from the cheaper and better market, or upon the changes of the weather, which may sometimes favour him by rendering a "trip to town" exceedingly undesirable.

FAILURES – "While the grass is growing the horse is starving"; and thus, while the new district is becoming peopled the funds of the small shopkeeper are gradually eaten up, and he puts up his shutters just at the time when a more cautious speculator steps in to profit by the connection already formed, and to take advantage of the now improved condition of the locality. It seems therefore desirable for the small capitalists rather to run the risk of a more expensive rent, in a well-peopled district, than to resort to places of slow and uncertain demand; for the welfare of the small shopkeeper depends entirely upon the frequency with which his limited stock is cleared out and replaced by fresh supplies.

PRECAUTIONS – But should the small capitalist still prefer opening in a suburban district, where competition is less severe, and rents and rates less burdensome, there are certain precautions which he will do well to observe. He should particularly guard against opening a shop to supply what may be termed the superfluities of life; for the inhabitants of suburban districts are those who, like himself, have resorted to a cheap residence for the sake of economy. Or, if this be not the case – if they are people of independent means, who prefer the "detached villa" to the town-house, squeezed up on both sides, they have the means of riding and driving to town, and will prefer choosing articles of taste and luxury from the best marts, enriched by the finest display.

NECESSITIES OR LUXURIES – The suburban shopkeeper should, therefore, confine himself to supplying the *necessities* of life. Hungry people dislike to fetch their bread from five miles off; and to bring vegetables from a long distance would evidently be a matter of considerable inconvenience. The baker, the butcher, the green-grocer, the beer retailer, &c., are those who find their successes first established in suburban localities. And not until these are doing well, should the tailor, the shoemaker, the hatter, the draper, the hosier, and others, expect to find return for their capital and reward for their labour.

CIVILITY – In larger localities, where competition abounds, the small shopkeeper frequently outstrips his more powerful rival by one element of success, which may be added to any stock without cost, but cannot be withheld without loss. That element is *civility*. It has already been spoken of elsewhere, but must be enforced here, as aiding the little means of the small shopkeeper to a wonderful degree. A kind and obliging manner carries with it an indescribable charm. It must not be a manner which indicates a mean, grovelling, time-serving spirit, but a plain, open, and agreeable demeanour, which seems to desire to oblige for the pleasure of doing so, and not for the sake of squeezing an extra penny out of a customer's pocket.

FAILURES OF LARGE SHOPKEEPERS – The large shopkeeper frequently grows proud of his position; there are many little civilities which customers like, but which the large shopkeeper may be too busy or unwilling to pay. He forgets that these civilities are the steps by which he rose, and that the withdrawal of them must lead to his rapid descent. Punctuality, cleanliness, the neat arrangement of the stock, the attractiveness of the window, the absence of all absurd puffing, the early and regular opening of the shop in the morning, and the attention paid to every one entering it – these are the secrets of the small shopkeeper's success against the influence of giant capital. They are a series of charms before which even gold itself must yield its potent influence.

INTEGRITY – The sole reliance of the shopkeeper should be in the integrity of his transactions, and in the civility of his demeanour. He should make it the interest and the pleasure of the customer to come to his shop. If he does this, he will find the very best "connections," and so long as he continues this system of business, they will never desert him.

DUTIES OF A SHOPKEEPER – He should cheerfully render his best labour and knowledge to serve those who approach his counter, and place confidence in his transactions; make himself alike to rich and poor, but never resort to mean subterfuge and deception to gain approbation and support. He should be frugal in his expenditure, that, in deriving profits from trade, he may not trespass unduly upon the interests of others; he should so hold the balance between man and man that he should feel nothing to reprove his conscience when the day comes for him to repose from his labours and live upon the fruits of his industry. Let the public discover such a man, and they will flock around him for their own sakes.

A VERY USEFUL BOOK, "The Shopkeeper's Guide" (published at half a crown), enlarges upon these subjects in a very able manner; and gives most useful hints to people in every department of trade.

DON'T RUN IN DEBT

"Don't run in debt:" – never mind, never mind,
If the clothes are faded and torn:
Seam them up, make them do; it is better by far,
Than to have the heart weary and worn.
Who'll love you the more for the shape of your hat,
Or your ruff, or the tie of your shoe.
The cut of your vest, or your boots, or cravat,
If they know you're in debt for the new.
There's no comfort, I tell you, in walking the street
In fine clothes if you know you are in debt;
And feel that perchance you some tradesman may meet,
Who will sneer – "They're not paid for yet."
Good friends, let me beg of you, don't run in debt,
If the chairs and the sofas are old –
They will fit your back better than any new set,
Unless they're paid for – with gold;
If the house is too small, draw the closer together,
Keep it warm with a hearty good will;
A big one unpaid for, in all kinds of weather,
Will send to your warm heart a chill.
Don't run in debt – now, dear girls, take a hint,
(If the fashions have changed since last season,)
Old Nature is out in the very same tint,
And old Nature, we think, has some reason.
But just say to your friend, that you cannot afford
To spend time to keep up with the fashion;
That your purse is too light, and your honour too bright,
To be tarnished with such silly passion.
Gents, don't run in debt – let your friends, if they can,
Have fine houses, feathers, and flowers,
But, unless they are paid for, be more of a man
Than to envy their sunshiny hours.
If you've money to spare, I have nothing to say –
Spend your silver and gold as you please;
But, mind you, the man who his bill has to pay
Is the man who is never at ease.
Kind husbands, don't run into debt any more;

'Twill fill your wife's cup full of sorrow,
To know that a neighbour may call at your door,
With a claim you must settle to-morrow.
Oh! take my advice – it is good, it is true!
(But, lest you may some of you doubt it,)
I'll whisper a secret, now seeing 'tis you –
I have tried it, and know all about it:
The chain of a debtor is heavy and cold,
Its links all corrosion and rust,
Gild it o'er as you will – it is never of gold,
Then spurn it aside with disgust.

A MORAL

I had a little spot of ground
Where blade nor blossom grew,
Though the bright sunshine all around
Life-giving radiance threw.
I mourn'd to see a spot so bare
Of leaves of healthful green,
And thought of bowers, and blossoms fair,
I frequently had seen.

Some seeds of various kinds lay by –
I knew not what they were –
But, rudely turning o'er the soil,
I strew'd them thickly there;
And day by day I watch'd them spring
From out the fertile earth,
And hoped for many a lovely thing
Of beauty and of worth.

But as I mark'd their leaves unfold
As weeds before my view,
And saw how stubbornly and bold
The thorns and nettles grew –
I sigh'd to think that I had done
Unwittingly, a thing,
That, where a beauteous bower should thrive,
But worthless weeds did bring.

And thus, I mused: the things we do
With little heed or ken,
May prove of worthless growth, and strew
With thorns the paths of men; –
For little deeds, like little seeds,
May flowers prove, or noxious weeds!

CHOICE OF FRIENDS – We should ever have it fixed in our memories, that *by the character of those whom we choose for our friends, our own is likely to be formed*, and will certainly be judged of by the world. We ought, therefore, to be slow and cautious in contracting intimacy; but when a virtuous friendship is once established, we must ever consider it as a sacred engagement. – *Dr. Blair.*

HINTS UPON PERSONAL MANNERS – It is sometimes objected to books upon etiquette that they cause those who consult them to act with mechanical restraint, and to show in society that they are governed by arbitrary rules, rather than by an intuitive perception of what is graceful and polite.

THIS OBJECTION IS UNSOUND, because it supposes that people who study the theory of etiquette do not also exercise their powers of observation in society, and obtain, by their intercourse with others, that freedom and ease of deportment, which society alone can impart.

BOOKS UPON ETIQUETTE are useful, inasmuch as that they expound the laws of polite society. Experience alone, however, can give effect to the precise *manner* in which those laws are required to be observed.

WHATEVER OBJECTIONS MAY BE raised to the teachings of works upon etiquette, there can be no sound argument against a series of simple and brief hints, which shall operate as precautions against mistakes in personal conduct.

AVOID INTERMEDDLING with the affairs of others. This is a most common fault. A number of people seldom meet but they begin discussing the affairs of some one who is absent. This is not only uncharitable but positively unjust. It is equivalent to trying a *cause in the absence of the person implicated*. Even in the criminal code a prisoner is presumed to be innocent until he is found guilty. Society, however, is less just, and passes judgment without hearing the defence. Depend upon it, as a certain rule, *that the people who unite with you in discussing the affairs of others will proceed to scandalise you the moment that you depart.*

BE CONSISTENT in the avowal of principles. Do not deny to-day that which you asserted yesterday. If you do, you will stultify yourself, and your opinions will soon to be found to have no weight. You may fancy that you gain favour by subserviency; but so far from gaining favour, you lose respect.

AVOID FALSEHOOD. There can be found no higher virtue than the love of truth. The man who deceives others must himself become the victim of morbid distrust. Knowing the deceit of his own heart, and the falsehood of his own tongue, his eyes must be always filled with suspicion, and he must lose the greatest of all happiness – confidence in those who surround him.

THE FOLLOWING ELEMENTS of manly character are worthy of frequent meditation:–
1. To be wise in his disputes.
2. To be a lamb in his home.
3. To be brave in battle and great in moral courage.
4. To be discreet in public.
5. To be a bard in his chair.
6. To be a teacher in his household.
7. To be a council in his nation.
8. To be an arbitrator in his vicinity.
9. To be a hermit in his church.
10. To be a legislator in his country.
11. To be conscientious in his actions.
12. To be happy in his life.
13. To be diligent in his calling.
14. To be just in his dealing.
15. That whatever he doeth be to the will of God.

AVOID MANIFESTATIONS OF ILL-TEMPER. Reason is given for man's guidance. Passion is the tempest by which reason is overthrown. Under the effects of passion man's mind becomes disordered, his face disfigured, his body deformed. A moment's passion has frequently cut off a life's friendship, destroyed a life's hope, embittered a life's peace, and brought unending sorrow and disgrace. It is scarcely worth while to enter into a comparative analysis of ill-temper and passion: they are alike discreditable, alike injurious, and should stand equally condemned.

AVOID PRIDE. If you are handsome, God made you so; if you are learned, some one instructed you; if you are rich, God gave you what you own. It is for others to perceive your goodness; but you should be blind to your own merits. There can be no comfort in deeming yourself better than you really are: that is self-deception. The best men throughout all history have been the most humble.

AFFECTATION IS A FORM OF PRIDE. It is, in fact, pride made ridiculous and contemptible. Some one writing upon affectation has remarked as follows:–

"If anything will sicken and disgust a man, it is the affected mincing way in which some people choose to talk. It is perfectly nauseous. If these young jackanapes who screw their words into all manner of diabolical shapes could only feel how perfectly disgusting they were, it might induce them to drop it. With many, it soon becomes such a confirmed habit, that they cannot again be taught to talk in a plain, straightforward, manly way. In the lower order of ladies' boarding-schools, and indeed, too much everywhere, the same sickening, mincing tone is too often found. Do, pray, good people, do talk in your natural tone, if you don't wish to be utterly ridiculous and contemptible."

WE HAVE ADOPTED THE FOREGOING paragraph because we approve of some of its sentiments, but chiefly because it shows that persons who object to affectation may go to the other extreme – vulgarity. It is vulgar, we think, to call even the most affected people "jackanapes, who screw their words into all manner of diabolical shapes." Avoid vulgarity in manner, in speech, and in correspondence. To conduct yourself vulgarly is to offer offence to those who are around you; to bring upon yourself the condemnation of persons of good taste; and to incur the penalty of exclusion from good society. Thus, cast among the vulgar, you become the victim of your own error.

AVOID SWEARING. An oath is but the wrath of a perturbed spirit.

IT IS *MEAN*. A man of high moral standing would rather treat an offence with contempt, than show his indignation by an oath.

IT IS *VULGAR*: altogether too low for a decent man.

IT IS *COWARDLY*: implying a fear either of not being believed or obeyed.

IT IS *UNGENTLEMANLY*. A gentleman, according to Webster, is a *genteelman* – well-bred, refined.

IT IS *INDECENT*: offensive to delicacy, and extremely unfit for human ears.

IT IS *FOOLISH*. "Want of decency is want of sense."

IT IS *ABUSIVE* – to the mind which conceives the oath, to the tongue which utters it, and to the person at whom it is aimed.

IT IS *VENOMOUS*, showing a man's heart to be as a nest of vipers; and every time he swears, one of them starts out from his head.

IT IS *CONTEMPTIBLE* – forfeiting the respect of all the wise and good.

IT IS *WICKED*: violating the Divine law, and provoking the displeasure of Him who will not hold him guiltless who takes His name in vain.

BE A GENTLEMAN – Moderation, decorum, and neatness, distinguish the gentleman; he is at all times affable, diffident, and studious to please. Intelligent and polite, his behaviour is pleasant and graceful. When he enters the dwelling of an inferior, he endeavours to hide, if possible, the difference between their ranks in life; ever willing to assist those around him, he is neither unkind, haughty, nor overbearing. In the mansions of the rich, the correctness of his mind induces him to bend to etiquette, but not to stoop to adulation; correct principle cautions him to avoid the gaming-table, inebriety, or any other foible that could occasion him self-reproach. Pleased with the pleasures of reflection, he rejoices to see the gaieties of society, and is fastidious upon no point of little import. – Appear only to be a gentleman, and its shadow will bring upon you contempt; be a gentleman, and its honours will remain even after you are dead.

THE TRUE GENTLEMAN

'Tis he whose every thought and deed
    By rule of virtue moves;
Whose generous tongue disdains to speak
    The thing his heart disproves.

Who never did a slander forge,
    His neighbour's fame to wound;
Nor to hearken to a false report,
    By malice whisper'd round.

Who vice, in all its pomp and power,
    Can treat with just neglect;
And piety, though clothed in rags,
    Religiously respect.

Who to his plighted words and trust
    Has ever firmly stood;
And, though he promised to his loss,
    He makes his promise good.

Whose soul in usury disdains
  His treasure to employ;
Whom no reward can ever bribe
  The guiltless to destroy.

BE HONEST. Not only because "honesty is the best policy," but because it is a duty to God and to man. The heart that can be gratified by dishonest gains; the ambition that can be satisfied by dishonest means; the mind that can be devoted to dishonest purposes, must be of the worst order.

HAVING LAID DOWN these general principles for the government of personal conduct, we will epitomise what we would still enforce:-

AVOID IDLENESS – it is the parent of many evils. Can you pray, "Give us this day our daily bread," and not hear the reply, "Do thou this day thy daily duty?"

AVOID TELLING IDLE TALES, which is like firing arrows in the dark: you know not into whose heart they may fall.

AVOID TALKING ABOUT YOURSELF; praising your own works; and proclaiming your own deeds. If they are good, they will proclaim themselves; if bad, the less you say of them the better.

AVOID ENVY, for it cannot benefit you, nor can it injure those against whom it is cherished.

AVOID DISPUTATION for the mere sake of argument. The man who disputes obstinately and in a bigoted spirit, is like the man who would stop the fountain from which he should drink. Earnest discussion is commendable; but factious argument never yet produced a good result.

BE KIND IN LITTLE THINGS. The true generosity of the heart is more displayed by deeds of minor kindness, than by acts which may partake of ostentation.

BE POLITE. Politeness is the poetry of conduct – and like poetry it has many qualities. Let not your politeness be too florid, but of that gentle kind which indicates refined nature.

BE SOCIABLE. Avoid reserve in society. Remember that the social elements, like the air we breathe, are purified by motion. Thought illumines thought, and smiles win smiles.

BE PUNCTUAL. One minute too late has lost many a golden opportunity. Besides which, the want of punctuality is an affront offered to the person to whom your presence is due.

THE FOREGOING REMARKS may be said to apply to the moral conduct, rather than to the details of personal manners. Great principles, however, suggest minor ones; and hence from the principles laid down many hints upon personal behaviour may be gathered.

BE HEARTY in your salutations.

BE DISCREET AND SINCERE in your friendships.

LIKE TO LISTEN rather than to talk.

BEHAVE, even in the presence of your relations, as though you felt respect to be due to them.

IN SOCIETY NEVER FORGET that you are but one of many.

WHEN YOU VISIT A FRIEND, conform to the rules of his home.

LEAN NOT UPON HIS TABLES, nor rub your feet against his chairs.

PRY NOT INTO LETTERS that are not your own.

PAY UNMISTAKEABLE respect to ladies everywhere.

BEWARE OF FOPPERY, and of silly flirtation.

AVOID DRUNKENNESS as you would a curse; and modify all appetites, especially those that are acquired.

DRESS WELL, but not superfluously.

BE NEITHER LIKE A SLOVEN, nor like a stuffed model.

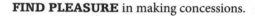

IN PUBLIC PLACES be not too pertinacious of your own rights.

FIND PLEASURE in making concessions.

SPEAK distinctly.

LOOK AT THE PERSON to whom you speak.

WHEN YOU HAVE SPOKEN, give him an opportunity to reply.

KEEP AWAY ALL UNCLEANLY appearances from the person. Let the nails, the teeth, and, in fact, the whole system receive *salutary* rather than *studied* care. But let these things receive attention at the toilette – not elsewhere.

AVOID DISPLAYING EXCESS of jewellery. Nothing looks more effeminate upon a man.

THE ART OF BEING AGREEABLE – The true art of being agreeable is to appear well pleased with all the company, and rather to seem well entertained with them than to bring entertainment to them. A man thus disposed, perhaps, may not have much learning, nor any wit; but if he has common sense, and something friendly in his behaviour, it conciliates men's minds more than the brightest parts without this disposition; and when a man of such a turn comes to old age, he is almost sure to be treated with respect. It is true, indeed, that we should not dissemble and flatter in company; but a man may be very agreeable, strictly consistent with truth and sincerity, by a prudent silence where he cannot concur, and a pleasing assent where he can.

THERE ARE MANY TALKERS, but few who know how to converse agreeably.

SPEAK DISTINCTLY, neither too rapidly nor too slowly.

ACCOMMODATE THE PITCH of your voice to the hearing of the person with whom you are conversing.

NEVER SPEAK with your mouth full.

TELL YOUR JOKES and laugh afterwards.

DISPENSE WITH SUPERFLUOUS WORDS – such as, "Well, I should think."

THE WOMAN WHO WISHES her conversation to be agreeable will avoid conceit or affectation, and laughter, which is not natural and spontaneous. Her language will be easy and unstudied, marked by a graceful carelessness, which, at the same time, never oversteps the limits of propriety. Her lips will readily yield to a pleasant smile; she will not love to hear herself talk; her tones will bear the impress of sincerity, and her eyes kindle with animation, as she speaks. The art of pleasing is, in truth, the very soul of good breeding; for the precise object of the latter is to render us agreeable to all with whom we associate: to make us, at the same time, esteemed and loved.

WE NEED SCARCELY ADVERT to the rudeness of interrupting any one who is speaking, or to the impropriety of pushing, to its full extent, a discussion which has become unpleasant.

SOME MEN HAVE A MANIA for Greek and Latin quotations; this is peculiarly to be avoided. It is like pulling up the stones from a tomb wherewith to kill the living. Nothing is more wearisome than pedantry.

IF YOU FEEL YOUR INTELLECTUAL superiority to any one with whom you are conversing, do not seek to bear him down; it would be an inglorious triumph, and a breach of good manners. Beware, too, of speaking lightly of subjects which bear a sacred character.

WITLINGS OCCASIONALLY gain a reputation in society; but nothing is more insipid and in worse taste than their conceited harangues and self-sufficient air.

IT IS A COMMON IDEA that the art of writing and the art of conversation are one; this is a great mistake. A man of genius may be a very dull talker.

THE TWO GRAND MODES of making your conversation interesting, are to enliven it by recitals calculated to affect and impress your hearers, and to intersperse it with anecdotes and smart things. Rivasol was a master in the latter mode.

CLEANLINESS – The want of cleanliness is a fault which admits of no excuse. Where water can be had for nothing, it is surely in the power of every person to be clean.

IF DIRTY PEOPLE CANNOT BE REMOVED as a common nuisance, they ought at least to be avoided as infectious. All who regard their health, should keep at a distance, even from their habitations.

EVEN OUR OWN FEELINGS are a sufficient proof of the necessity of cleanliness. How refreshed, how cheerful and agreeable does one feel on being shaved, washed, and dressed; especially when these have been long neglected.

MOST PEOPLE esteem cleanliness; and even those who do not practise it themselves, often admire it in others.

CLEANLINESS – "I have more than once expressed my conviction that the humanizing influence of habits of cleanliness and of those decent observations which imply self-respect – the best, indeed the only foundation of respect for others – has never been sufficiently acted on. A clean, fresh, and well-ordered house exercises over its inmates a moral no less than a physical influence, and has a direct tendency to make the members of a family sober, peaceable, and considerate of the feelings and happiness of each other; nor is it difficult to trace a connection between habitual feelings of this sort and the formation of habits of respect for property, for the laws in general, and even for those higher duties and obligations the observance of which no laws can enforce." – *Dr. Southwood Smith.*

SUPERFLUOUS HAIR – Any remedy is doubtful; many of those commonly used are dangerous. The safest plan is as follows:– The hairs should be perseveringly plucked up by the roots, and the skin, having been washed twice a day with warm soft water, without soap, should be treated with the following wash, commonly called *Milk of Roses*. – Beat four ounces of sweet almonds in a mortar, and add half an ounce of white sugar during the process; reduce the whole to a paste by pounding; then add, in small quantities at a time, eight ounces of rose water. The emulsion thus formed, should be strained through a fine cloth, and the residue again pounded, while the strained fluid should be bottled in a large stopped vial. To the pasty mass in the mortar add

half an ounce of sugar, and eight ounces of rose water, and strain again. This process must be repeated three times. To the thirty-two ounces of fluid, add twenty grains of the bichloride of mercury, dissolved in two ounces of alcohol, and shake the mixture for five minutes. The fluid should be applied with a towel, immediately after washing, and the skin gently rubbed with a dry cloth

till *perfectly* dry. Wilson, in his work on *Healthy Skin*, writes as follows:–
"Substances are sold by the perfumers called depilatories, which are
represented as having the power of removing hair. But the hair is not
destroyed by these means, the root and that part of the shaft implanted
within the skin still remain, and are ready to shoot up with increased
vigour as soon as the depilatory is withdrawn. The effect of the
depilatory is the same, in this respect, as that of a razor, and the latter
is, unquestionably, the better remedy. It must not, however, be
imagined that depilatories are negative remedies, and that, if they do
no permanent good, they are, at least, harmless; that is not the fact,
they are violent irritants, and require to be used with the utmost
caution. After all, the safest depilatory is a pair of tweezers and
patience."

THE YOUNG LADY'S TOILETTE

Self-Knowledge – The Enchanting Mirror
This curious glass will bring your faults to light,
And make your virtues shine both strong and bright.

Contentment – Wash to smooth Wrinkles
A daily portion of this essence use,
'Twill smooth the brow, and tranquillity infuse.

Truth – Fine Lip-salves
Use daily for your lips this precious dye,
They'll redden, and breathe sweet melody.

Prayer – Mixture, giving Sweetness to the Voice
At morning, noon, and night, this mixture take,
Your tones improved, will richer music make.

Compassion – Best Eye-water
These drops will add great lustre to the eye;
When more you need, the poor will you supply.

Wisdom – Solutions to prevent Eruptions
It calms the temper, beautifies the face,
And gives to woman dignity and grace.

Attention and Obedience – Matchless Pair of Ear-rings
With these clear drops appended to the ear,
Attentive lessons you will gladly hear.

Neatness and Industry – Indispensable Pair of Bracelets
Clasp them on carefully each day you live,
To good designs they efficacy give.

Patience – An Elastic Girdle
The more you use the brighter it will grow,
Though its least merit is external show.

Principle – Ring of Tried Gold
Yield not this golden bracelet while you live,
'Twill sin restrain and peace of conscience give.

Resignation – Necklace of Purest Pearl
This ornament embellishes the fair,
And teaches all the ills of life to bear.

Love – Diamond Breast-pins
Adorn your bosom with this precious pin,
It shines without, and warms the heart within.

Politeness – A Graceful Bandeau
The forehead neatly circled with this band,
Will admiration and respect command.

Piety – A Precious Diadem
Whoe'er this precious diadem shall own,
Secures herself an everlasting crown.

Good Temper – Universal Beautifier
With this choice liquid gently touch the mouth,
It spreads o'er all the face the charms of youth.

HOW TO GET SLEEP – How to get sleep is to many persons a matter of high importance. Nervous persons, who are troubled with wakefulness and excitability, usually have a strong tendency of blood on the brain, with cold extremities. The pressure of the blood on the brain keeps it in a stimulated or wakeful state, and the pulsations in the head are often painful. Let such rise and chafe the body and extremities with a brush or towel, or rub smartly with the hands, to promote circulation, and withdraw the excessive amount of blood from the brain, and they will fall asleep in a few moments. A cold bath, or a sponge bath and rubbing, or a good run, or a rapid walk in the open air, or going up and down stairs a few times just before retiring, will aid in equalising circulation and promoting sleep. These rules are simple and easy of application in castle or cabin, and may minister to the comfort of thousands who would freely expend money for an anodyne to promote "Nature's sweet restorer, balmy sleep!"

EXERCISE – Three principal points in the manner of taking exercise are necessary to be attended to:– 1. The kind of exercise. 2. The proper time for exercise. 3. The duration of it. With respect to the kinds of exercise, the various species of it may be divided into active and passive. Among the first, which admit of being considerably diversified, may be enumerated walking, running, leaping, swimming, riding, fencing, the military exercise, different sorts of athletic games, &c. Among the latter, or passive kinds of exercise, may be comprised riding in a carriage, sailing, friction, swinging, &c.

THE FIRST, or active exercises, are more beneficial to youth, to the middle-aged, to the robust in general, and particularly to the corpulent and the plethoric.

THE SECOND, or passive kinds of exercise, on the contrary, are better calculated for children; old, dry, and emaciated persons of a delicate and debilitated constitution; and particularly to the asthmatic and consumptive.

THE TIME at which exercise is most proper, depends on such a variety of concurrent circumstances, that it does not admit of being regulated by any general rules, and must therefore be collected from the observations made on the effects of air, food, drink, &c.

WITH RESPECT TO THE DURATION OF EXERCISE, there are other particulars, relative to a greater or lesser degree of fatigue attending the different species, and utility of it in certain states of the mind and body, which must determine this consideration as well as the preceding.

THAT EXERCISE IS TO BE PREFERRED which, with a view to brace and strengthen the body, we are most accustomed to, as any unusual one may be attended with a contrary effect.

EXERCISE SHOULD BE BEGUN and finished gradually, never abruptly.

EXERCISE IN THE OPEN AIR has many advantages over that used within doors.

TO CONTINUE EXERCISE until a profuse perspiration or a great degree of weariness takes place, is far from being wholesome.

IN THE FORENOON, when the stomach is not too much distended, muscular motion is both agreeable and healthful; it strengthens digestion, and heats the body less than with a full stomach; and a good appetite after it is a proof that it has not been carried to excess. But, at the same time, it should be understood, that it is not advisable to take violent exercise immediately before a meal, as digestion might thereby be retarded.

NEITHER should we sit down to a substantial dinner or supper immediately on returning from a fatiguing walk, at a time when the blood is heated, and the body in a state of perspiration from previous exertion, as the worst consequences may arise, especially where cooling dishes, salad, or a glass of cold drink is begun with.

EXERCISE IS ALWAYS HURTFUL AFTER MEALS, from its impeding digestion, by propelling those fluids too much towards the surface of the body which are designed for the solution of the food in the stomach.

SWIMMING – Every person, male and female, should endeavour to acquire the power of swimming. The fact that the exercise is a healthful accompaniment of bathing, and that lives may be saved by it, even when least expected, is a sufficient argument for the recommendation. The art of swimming is, in fact, very easy, and those persons who take the few brief hints we are about to offer, will soon find themselves rewarded by complete success. The first consideration is not to attempt to learn to swim too soon. That is to say, you must not expect to succeed in your efforts to swim, until you have become accustomed to the water, and have overcome your repugnance to the coldness and novelty of bathing. Every attempt will fail until you have acquired a certain confidence in the water, and then the difficulty will soon vanish. When this confidence has been gained, the following hints by the celebrated Dr. Franklin will be found all that can be required:–

DR. FRANKLIN'S ADVICE TO SWIMMERS – "The only obstacle to improvement in this necessary and life-preserving art, is fear; and it is only by overcoming this timidity that you can expect to become a master of the following acquirements. It is very common for novices in the art of swimming to make use of corks or bladders to assist in keeping the body above water: some have utterly condemned the use of them; however, they may be of service for supporting the body, while one is learning what is called the stroke, or that manner of drawing in and striking out the hands and feet, that is necessary to produce progressive motion. But you will be no swimmer till you can place confidence in the power of the water to support you; I would, therefore, advise the acquiring that confidence in the first place; especially as I have known several, who, by a little practice necessary for that purpose, have insensibly acquired the stroke, taught as it were by nature. The practice I mean is this: choosing a place where the water deepens gradually, walk coolly into it till it is up to your breast; then turn round your face to the shore, and throw an egg into the water between you and the shore; it will sink to the bottom, and be easily seen there if the water be clear. It must lie in the water so deep that you cannot reach to take it up but by diving for it. To encourage yourself, in order to do this, reflect that your progress will be from deep to shallow water, and that at any time you may, by bringing your legs under you, and standing on the bottom, raise your head far above the water; then plunge under it with your eyes open, which must be kept open before going under, as you cannot open the eyelids for the weight of water above you; throwing yourself toward the egg, and endeavouring, by the action of your hands and feet against the water, to get forward, till within reach of it. In this attempt you will find that the water buoys you up against your inclination; that it is not so easy to sink as you imagine, and that you cannot, but by active force, get down to the egg. Thus you feel the power of water to support you, and learn to confide in that power, while your endeavours to overcome it, and reach the egg, teach you the manner of acting on the water with your feet and hands, which action is afterwards used in swimming to support your head higher above the water, or to go forward through it.

"**I WOULD THE MORE EARNESTLY** press you to the trial of this method, because, I think I shall satisfy you that your body is lighter than water, and that you might float in it a long time with your mouth free for breathing, if you would put yourself into a proper posture, and would be still, and forbear struggling; yet, till you have obtained this experimental confidence in the water, I cannot depend upon your having the necessary presence of mind to recollect the posture, and the directions I gave you relating to it. The surprise may put all out of your mind.

"**THOUGH THE LEGS**, arms, and head of a human body, being solid parts, are, specifically, somewhat heavier than fresh water, as the trunk, particularly the upper part, for its hollowness, is so much lighter than water, as that the whole of the body, taken altogether, is too light to sink wholly under water, but some part will remain above, until the lungs become filled with water, which happens from drawing water to them instead of air, when a person, in the fright, attempts breathing, while the mouth and nostrils are under water.

"**THE LEGS AND ARMS** are specifically lighter than salt water, and will be supported by it, so that a human body cannot sink in salt water, though the lungs were filled as above, but from the greater specific gravity of the head. Therefore, a person throwing himself on his back in salt water, and extending his arms, may easily lay so as to keep his mouth and nostrils free for breathing; and, by a small motion of his hand, may prevent turning, if he should perceive any tendency to it.

"**IN FRESH WATER**, if a man throw himself on his back, near the surface, he cannot long continue in that situation but by proper action of his hands on the water; if he use no such action, the legs and lower part of the body will gradually sink till he come into an upright position, in which he will continue suspended, the hollow of his breast keeping the head uppermost.

"**BUT IF, IN THIS ERECT POSITION**, the head be kept upright above the shoulders, as when we stand on the ground, the immersion will, by the weight of that part of the head that is out of the water, reach above the mouth and nostrils, perhaps a little above the eyes, so that a man cannot long remain suspended in water, with his head in that position.

"**THE BODY CONTINUING SUSPENDED** as before, and upright, if the head be leaned quite back, so that the face look upward, all the back part of the head being under water, and its weight, consequently, in a great measure supported by it, the face will remain above water quite free for breathing, will rise an inch higher every inspiration, and sink as much every expiration, but never so low as that the water may come over the mouth.

"**IF, THEREFORE, A PERSON UNACQUAINTED** with swimming, and falling accidentally into the water, could have presence of mind sufficient to avoid struggling and plunging, and to let the body take this natural position, he might continue long safe from drowning, till, perhaps, help should come; for, as to the clothes, their additional weight when immersed is very inconsiderable, the water supporting it; though, when he comes out of the water, he will find them very heavy indeed.

"**BUT, AS I SAID BEFORE**, I would not advise you, or any one, to depend on having this presence of mind on such an occasion, but learn fairly to swim, as I wish all men were taught to do in their youth; they would, on many occasions, be the safer for having that skill; and, on many more, the happier, as free from painful apprehensions of danger, to say nothing of the enjoyment in so delightful and wholesome an exercise. Soldiers particularly should, methinks, all be taught to swim; it might be of frequent use, either in surprising an enemy or saving themselves; and if I had now boys to educate, I should prefer those schools (other things being equal) where an opportunity was afforded for acquiring so advantageous an art, which, once learned, is never forgotten.

"**I KNOW BY EXPERIENCE**, that it is a great comfort to a swimmer, who has a considerable distance to go, to turn himself sometimes on his back, and to vary, in other respects, the means of procuring a progressive motion.

"**WHEN HE IS SEIZED WITH THE CRAMP** in the leg, the method of driving it away is, to give the parts affected a sudden, vigorous, and violent shock; which he may do in the air as he swims on his back.

"**DURING THE GREAT HEATS** in summer there is no danger in bathing, however warm we may be, in rivers which have been thoroughly warmed by the sun. But to throw one's-self into cold spring water, when the body has been heated by exercise in the sun, is an imprudence which may prove fatal. I once knew an instance of four young men, who, having worked at harvest in the heat of the day, with a view of refreshing themselves, plunged into a spring of cold water;

two died upon the spot, a third next morning, and the fourth recovered with great difficulty. A copious draught of cold water, in similar circumstances, is frequently attended with the same effect, in North America.

"**THE EXERCISE OF SWIMMING** is one of the most healthy and agreeable in the world. After having swam for an hour or two in the evening, one sleeps coolly the whole night, even during the most ardent heats of summer. Perhaps the pores being cleansed, the insensible perspiration increases and occasions this coolness. It is certain that much swimming is the means of stopping diarrhoea, and even of producing a constipation. With respect to those who do not know how to swim, or who are affected with a diarrhoea at a season which does not permit them to use that exercise, a warm bath, by cleansing and purifying the skin, is found very salutary, and often effects a radical cure. I speak from my own experience, frequently repeated, and that of others to whom I have recommended this.

"**WHEN I WAS A BOY**, I amused myself one day with flying a paper kite; and approaching the banks of a lake, which was near a mile broad, I tied the string to a stake, and the kite ascended to a very considerable height above the pond, while I was swimming. In a little time, being desirous of amusing myself with my kite, and enjoying at the same time the pleasure of swimming, I returned, and loosening from the stake the string with the little stick which was fastened to it, went again into the water, where I found that, lying on my back and holding the stick in my hand, I was drawn along the surface of the water in a very agreeable manner. Having then engaged another boy to carry my clothes round the pond, to a place which I pointed out to him, on the other side, I began to cross the pond with my kite, which carried me quite over without the least fatigue, and with the greatest pleasure imaginable. I was only obliged occasionally to halt a little in my course, and resist its progress, when it appeared that, by following too quick, I lowered the kite too much; by doing which occasionally I made it rise again. I have never since that time practised this singular mode of swimming, though I think it not impossible to cross, in this manner, from Dover to Calais. The packet-boat, however, is still preferable."

ERRORS IN SPEAKING – There are several kinds of errors in speaking. The most objectionable of them are those in which words are employed that are unsuitable to convey the meaning intended. Thus, a person wishing to express his intention of going to a given place, says, "I *propose* going," when, in fact, he *purposes* going. An amusing illustration of this class of error was overheard by ourselves. A venerable matron was speaking of her son, who, she said, was quite stagestruck. "In fact," remarked the old lady, "he is going to a *premature* performance this evening!" Considering that most *amateur* performances are *premature*, we hesitate to say that this word was misapplied; though, evidently, the maternal intention was to convey quite another meaning.

OTHER ERRORS ARISE from the substitution of sounds similar to the words which should be employed. That is, spurious words instead of genuine ones. Thus, some people say "*renumerative*," when they mean "*remunerative*." A nurse, recommending her mistress to have one of the newly-invented carriages for her child, advised her to purchase a *preamputator*!

OTHER ERRORS ARE OCCASIONED by imperfect knowledge of the English grammar. Thus, many people say, "Between you and *I*," instead of "Between you and *me*." By the misuse of the adjective: "What *beautiful* butter," "What a *nice* landscape." They should say, "What a *beautiful landscape*," "What *nice butter*." And by numerous other departures from the rules of grammar, which will be pointed out hereafter.

BY THE MISPRONUNCIATION of words. Many persons say *pronounciation* instead of *pronunciation*; others say pro-nun`-she-a-shun, instead of pro-nun-ce-a-shun.

BY THE MISDIVISION of words and syllables. This defect makes the words *an ambassador* sound like *a nam-bassador*, or *an adder* like *a nadder*.

BY IMPERFECT ENUNCIATION, as when a person says *hebben* for *heaven*, *ebber* for *ever*, *jocholate* for *chocolate*, *a hedge*, *a nedge*, or *an edge*, *a hedge*.

BY THE USE OF PROVINCIALISMS, or words retained from various dialects, of which we give the following examples:–

Cambridgeshire, Cheshire, Suffolk, &c.
Foyne, twoyne, for *fine*, *twine*; ineet for *night*; ă-mon for *man*; poo for *pull*.

Cumberland, Scotland, &c.
Cuil, bluid, for *cool*, *blood*; spwort, scworn, whoam, for *sport*, *scorn*, *home*; a-theere for *there*; ĕ-reed, seven, for *red*, *seven*; bleedin for *bleeding*; hawf for *half*; saumon for *salmon*.

Devonshire, Cornwall, &c.
F-vind for *find*; fet for *fetch*; wid for *with*; zee for *see*; tudder for *the other*; drash, droo, for *thrash*, and *through*; gewse for *goose*; Toosday for *Tuesday*.

Essex, London, &c.
V-wiew for *view*; went for *vent*; vite for *white*; ven for *when*; vot for *what*.

Hereford, &c.
Clom for *climb*; hove for *heave*; puck for *pick*; rep for *reap*; sled for *sledge*.

Leicestershire, Lincolnshire, Lancashire, &c.
Housen for houses; a-loyne for *lane*; mon for *man*; thik for *this*; brig for *bridge*; thack, pick, for *thatch*, *pitch*.

Yorkshire, &c.
Foyt for *foot*; foight for *fight*; o-noite, foil, coil, hoil, for *note, foal, coal, hole*; loyne for *lane*; o-nooin, gooise, fooil, tooil, for *noon, goose, fool, tool*; spwort, scworn, whoam, for *sport, scorn, home*; g-yet for *gate*.

THE FOLLOWING EXAMPLES of provincial dialects will be found very amusing:–

The Cornwall School-boy
An ould man found, one day, a young gentleman's portmantle, as he were a going to es dennar; he took'd et en and gived et to es wife, and said "Mally, here's a roul of lither, look, see, I suppoase some poor ould shoemaker or other have los'en, tak'en, and put'en a top of the teaster of tha bed, he'll be glad to hab'en agin sum day, I dear say." The ould man, Jan, that was es neame, went to es work as before. Mally than opened the portmantle, and found en et three hunderd pounds. Soon after thes, the ould man not being very well, Mally said, "Jan, I'ave saaved away a little money, by the bye, and as thee caan't read or write, thee shu'st go to school" (he were then nigh threescore and ten). He went but a very short time, and comed hoam one day and said, "Mally, I waint go to scool no more, 'caase the childer do be laffen at me; they can tell their letters, and I caan't tell my A, B, C, and I wud rather go to work agen." "Do as thee wool," ses Mally. Jan had not been out many days, afore the young gentleman came by that lost the portmantle, and said, "Well, my ould man, did'ee see or hear tell o' sich a thing as a portmantle?" "Portmantle, sar, was't that un, sumthing like thickey?" (pointing to one behind es saddle). I vound one the to'thr day zackly like that." "Where es et?" "Come along, I carr'den and gov'en to my ould 'ooman, Mally; thee sha't av'en, nevr vear. Mally, where es that roul of lither I broft en tould thee to put en a top of the teaster of the bed, *afore I go'd to scool?*" "Drat thee emperance," said the young gentleman, "thee art bewattled; *that were afore I were born.*" So he druv'd off, and left all the three hunderd pounds with Jan an Mally.

The Middlesex Thimblerigger
Now, then, my jolly sportsmen, I've got more money than the parson of the parish. Those as don't play can't vin, and those as are here harnt there! I'd hold any on you, from a tanner to a sovereign, or ten, as you don't tell which thimble the pea is under." "It's there, Sir." "I barr tellings." "I'll go it again." "Vat you don't see don't look at, and vat you do see don't tell. I'll hould you a soveren, Sir, you don't tell me vitch thimble the pea is under." "Lay him, Sir, (in a whisper) it's under the

middle 'un. I'll go you halves." "Lay him another; that's right." "I'm blow'd but we've lost; who'd a thought it?" Smack goes the flat's hat over his eyes; exit the confederates, with a loud laugh.

The Harnet and the Bittle – Wiltshire
A harnet zet in a hollur tree,–
A proper spiteful twoad was he;
And a merrily zung while he did zet
His stinge as shearp as a bagganet;
"Oh, who so vine and bowld as I,
I vears not bee, nor waspe, nor vly."

A bittle up thuck tree did clim,
And scornfully did look at him;
Zays he, "Zur harnet, who giv thee
A right to zet in thuck there tree?
Vor ael you zings zo nation vine,
I tell 'e 'tis a house o' mine."

The harnet's conscience velt a twinge,
But grawin' bowld wi his long stinge,
Zays he, "Possession's the best laaw;
Zo here th' sha'snt put a claaw!
Be off, and leave the tree to me,
The mixen's good enough for thee!"

Just then a yuckel passin' by,
Was axed by them the cause to try:
"Ha! ha! I zee how 'tis!" zays he,
"They'll make a vamous munch vor me!"
His bill was shearp, his stomach lear,
Zo up a snapped the caddlin pair!

MORAL
All you as be to laaw inclined,
This leetle stowry bear in mind;
Vor if to laaw you aims to gwo,
You'll vind thy'll allus zar'e zo:
You'll meet the vate o' these here two,
They'll take your cwoat and carcass too!

Yorkshire
Men an' women is like so monny cards, played wi' be two oppoanents, Time an' Eternity: Time gets a gam noo an' then, and hez t'pleasure o' keepin' his cards for a bit, bud Eternity's be far t'better hand, an' proves, day be day, an' hoor be hoor, 'at he's winnin' incalcalably fast.

"Hoo sweet, hoo varry sweet is life!" as t' flee said when he wur stuck i' treacle!

PERSONS BRED IN THESE localities, and in Ireland and Scotland, retain more or less of their provincialisms; and, therefore, when they move into other districts they become conspicuous for the peculiarities of their speaking. In many cases they appear vulgar and uneducated, when they are not so. It is, therefore, very desirable for all persons to approach the recognised standard of correctness as nearly as possible.

TO CORRECT THESE ERRORS by a systematic course of study, would involve a closer application than our readers generally could afford; and would require much more space than we can devote to the subject. We will therefore give numerous rules and hints, in a concise and simple form, which will be of great assistance to Enquirers.

These Rules and Hints will be founded upon the authority of scholars, the usages of the bar, the pulpit, and the senate, and the authority of societies formed for the purpose of collecting and diffusing knowledge pertaining to the language of this country.

Who and *whom* are used in relation to persons, and *which* in relation to things. But it was once common to say "the man *which*." This should now be avoided. It is now usual to say, "Our Father *who* art in heaven," instead of "*which* art in heaven."

Whose, is, however, sometimes applied to things as to persons. We may, therefore, say, "the country *whose* inhabitants are free." [Grammarians differ in opinion upon this subject, but general usage justifies the rule.]

Thou is employed in solemn discourse, and *you* in common language. *Ye* (plural) is also used in serious addresses, and *you*, in familiar language.

The uses of the word *It* are various, and very perplexing to the uneducated. It is not only used to imply persons, but things, and even ideas, and therefore, in speaking or writing, its assistance is constantly required. The perplexity respecting this word arises from the fact that in using it in the construction of a long sentence, sufficient care is not taken to ensure that when *it* is employed it really points out or refers to the object intended. For instance, "It was raining when John set out in his cart to go to the market, and he was delayed so long that it was over before he arrived." Now what is to be understood by this sentence? Was the rain over? or the market? Either or both might be inferred from the construction of the sentence, which, therefore, should be written thus:– "It was raining when John set out in his cart, to go to the market, and he was delayed so long that the market was over before he arrived."

Rule – After writing a sentence always look through it, and see that wherever the word *It* is employed, it refers to or carries the mind back to the object which it is intended to point out.

The general distinction between *This* and *That*, is, *this* denotes an object present or near, in time or place, *that* to be absent.

These refers, in the same manner, to present objects, while *those* refers to things that are remote.

Who changes, under certain conditions, into *whose* and *whom*. But *that* and *which* always remain the same.

That may be applied to nouns or subjects of all sorts, as, the *girl that* went to school, the *dog that* bit me, the *ship that* went to London, the *opinion that* he entertains.

The misuse of these pronouns gives rise to more errors in speaking and writing than any other cause.

When you wish to distinguish between two or more persons say, "*Which* is the happy man?" – not *who* – "*Which* of those ladies do you admire?"

Instead of "*Who* do you think him to be?" – Say "*whom* do you think him to be?"

Whom should I see?

To *whom* do you speak?

Who said so?

Who gave it to you?

Of whom did you procure them?

Who was *he*?

Who do men say that *I* am?

Whom do they represent *me* to be?

In many instances in which *who* is used as an interrogative, it does not become *whom*; as "*Who* do you speak to?" "*Who* do you expect?" "*Who* is she married to?" "*Who* is this reserved for?" "*Who* was it made by?" Such sentences are found in the writings of our best authors, and it would be presumptuous to consider them as ungrammatical. If the word *whom* should be preferred, then it would be best to say, "For *whom* is this reserved?" &c.

Self should never be added to *his*, *their*, *mine*, or *thine*.

Each is used to denote every individual of a number.

Every denotes all the individuals of a number.

Either and *or* denotes an alternative: "I will take *either* road, at your pleasure;" "I will take this *or* that."

Neither means *not either*; and *nor* means *not other*.

Either is sometimes used for *each* – "Two thieves were crucified, on *either* side one."

Do not use double comparatives, such as *most straightest, most highest, most finest*.

The term *worser* has gone out of use; but *lesser* is still retained.

The use of such words as *chiefest, extremest*, &c., has become obsolete, because they do not give any superior force to the meanings of the primary words, *chief, extreme*, &c.

Such expressions as *more impossible, more indispensable, more universal, more uncontrollable, more unlimited*, &c., are objectionable, as they really enfeeble the meaning which it is the object of the speaker or writer to strengthen. For instance, *impossible* gains no strength by rendering it *more* impossible. This class of error is common with persons who say, "A *great large* house," "A *great big* animal," "A *little small* foot," "A *tiny little* hand."

Here, *there*, and *where*, originally denoting place, may now, by common consent, be used to denote other meanings; such as, "*There* I agree with you," "*Where* we differ," "We find pain *where* we expected pleasure," "*Here* you mistake me."

Hence, *whence*, and *thence*, denoting departure, &c., may be used without the word *from*. The idea of *from* is included in the word *whence* – therefore it is unnecessary to say, "*From whence*."

Hither, *thither*, and *whither*, denoting *to* a place, have generally been superseded by *here*, *there*, and *where*. But there is no good reason why they should not be employed. If, however, they are used, it is unnecessary to add the word *to*, because that is implied – "*Whither* are you going?" "*Where* are you going?" Each of these sentences is complete. To say, "Where are you going *to*?" is redundant.

Two *negatives* destroy each other, and produce an affirmative. "*Nor* did he *not* observe them," conveys the idea that he *did* observe them."

But negative assertions are allowable. "His manners are not unpolite," which implies that his manners are, in some degree, marked by politeness.

Instead of "I doubt not *but* I shall be able to go," say "I doubt not that I shall be able to go."

When asked "Who is there?" do not answer "*Me*," but "I."

Instead of "For you and *I*," say "For you and me."

Instead of "*Says I*," say "I said."

Instead of "I *ayn't*," or, "I *aren't*," say "I am not."

It is better to say "Bred and born," than "Born and bred."

It is better to say "A physician," or "A surgeon" (according to his degree), than "A medical man."

Instead of "He was too young to *have* suffered much," say "He was too young to suffer much."

Instead of "*Less* friends," say "Fewer friends." Less refers to quantity.

Instead of "If I am *not mistaken*," say "If I mistake not."

Instead of "What *beautiful* tea," say "What good tea."

Instead of "What a *nice* prospect," say "What a beautiful prospect."

Instead of "I hope you'll think nothing *on* it," say "I hope you'll think nothing of it."

Instead of "I suspect the *veracity* of his story," say "I doubt the truth of his story."

Instead of "*Rather warmish*," or "A *little* warmish," say "Rather warm."

Instead of "*Shay*," say "Chaise."

Instead of "He is a very *rising* person," say "He is rising rapidly."

Instead of "Who *learns* you music?" say "Who teaches you music?"

Instead of saying "The *observation* of the rule," say "The observance of the rule."

Instead of "Here *lays* his honoured head," say "Here lies his honoured head."

Instead of "He died from *negligence*," say "He died through neglect," or "in consequence of neglect."

Instead of "Apples are plenty," say "Apples are plentiful."

Instead of "For *ought* I know," say, "For aught I know."

Instead of "*Two couples*," say "Four persons."

But you may say "A married couple," or, "A married pair," or, "A couple of fowls," &c., in any case where one of each sex is to be understood.

Instead of "They are *united together* in the bonds of matrimony," say "They are united in matrimony," or, "They are married."

Instead of "We travel *slow*," say "We travel slowly."

Instead of "He is *noways* to blame," say "He is nowise to be blamed."

Instead of "He jumped *from off of* the scaffolding," say "He jumped off from the scaffolding."

Instead of "A *large enough* room," say "A room large enough."

Instead of "I went *for* to see him," say "I went to see him."

Instead of "The cake is all *eat up*," say "The cake is all eaten."

Instead of "It is bad *at the best*," say "It is very bad."

Instead of "Handsome is *as* handsome does," say "Handsome is who handsome does."

Instead of "Captain Reilly was killed *by* a bullet," say "Captain Reilly was killed with a bullet."

Instead of "A sad curse is war," say "War is a sad curse."

Instead of "His health was *drank with enthusiasm*," say "His health was drunk enthusiastically."

Instead of "It grieves me to see you," say "I am grieved to see you."

Instead of "Give me *them* papers," say "Give me those papers."

Instead of "He *belongs* to the Reform Club," say "He is a member of the Reform Club."

Avoid such phrases as "I am up to you," "I'll be down upon you," "Cut," or "Mizzle."

Instead of "I *should just* think I could," say "I think I can."

Instead of "Your *obedient, humble servant*," say "Your obedient," or "Your humble servant."

Dispense with the phrase "*Conceal from themselves the fact*." It suggests a gross anomaly.

Never say "*Pure and unadulterated*," because the phrase embodies a repetition.

Instead of saying "Charlotte was met *with* Thomas," say "Charlotte was met by Thomas." But if Charlotte and Thomas were walking together, "Charlotte and Thomas were met by," &c.

Instead of "It is strange that no author should *never* have written," say "It is strange that no author should ever have written."

Instead of "I won't never write," say "I will never write."

To say "Do *not* give him *no more* of your money," is equivalent to saying "Give him *some* of your money." Say "Do not give him any of your money."

Instead of saying, "I had not the pleasure of *hearing* his sentiments when I wrote that letter," say "I had not the pleasure of having heard," &c.

Instead of "The quality of the apples *were* good," say "The quality of the apples was good."

Instead of "We called *at* William," say "We called on William."

Instead of "Is Lord Palmerston *in*?" say "Is Lord Palmerston within?"

Instead of "She said, says she," say "She said."

Avoid such phrases as "I said, says I," "Thinks I to myself, thinks I," &c.

Instead of "He was in *eminent* danger," say "He was in imminent danger."

Instead of "I *sweat*," say "I perspire."

Avoid such exclamations as "God bless me!" "God deliver me!" "By God!" "By Gor'!" "My Lor'!" "Upon my soul!" &c.

"THOU SHALT NOT TAKE THE NAME OF THE LORD THY GOD IN VAIN."

PRONUNCIATION – Accent is a particular stress or force of the voice upon certain syllables or words. This mark ` in printing denotes the syllable upon which the stress or force of the voice should be placed.

A WORD may have more than one accent. Take as an instance as`-pira`-tion. In uttering this word we give a marked emphasis of the voice upon the first and third syllables, and therefore those syllables are said to be accented. The first of these accents is less distinguishable than the second, upon which we dwell longer, therefore the second accent is called the primary, or chief accent of the word.

WHEN the full accent falls on a vowel, that vowel should have a long sound, as in *vo`cal*; but when it falls on a consonant, the preceding vowel has a short sound, as in *hab`it*.

TO OBTAIN a good knowledge of pronunciation, it is advisable for the reader to listen to the examples given by good speakers, and by educated persons. We learn the pronunciation of words, to a great extent, by *imitation*, just as birds acquire the notes of other birds which may be near them.

BUT it will be very important to bear in mind that there are many words having a double meaning or application, and that the difference of meaning is indicated by the difference of the accent. Among these words, *nouns* are distinguished from *verbs* by this means: *Nouns* are accented on the first syllable, and verbs on the last.

NOUN signifies name; *nouns* are the names of persons and things; as well as of things not material and palpable, but of which we have a conception and knowledge, such as *courage, firmness, goodness, strength*; and *verbs* express *actions, movements*, &c. If the word used signifies that anything has been done, or is being done, or is, or is to be done, – then that word is a *verb*.

THUS, when we say that anything is "an in`sult," that word is a *noun*, and is accented on the first syllable; but when we say he did it "to insult` another person," the word insult` implies *acting*, and becomes a verb, and should be accented on the last syllable. The effect is, that, in speaking, you should employ a different pronunciation in the use of the same word, when uttering such sentences as these:– "What an in`sult!" "Do you mean to insult` me?" In the first instance you would lay the stress of voice upon the *in`*, and in the latter case upon the *sult`*.

HINTS TO "COCKNEY" SPEAKERS

The most objectionable error of the Cockney, that of substituting the *v* for the *w*, and *vice versa*, is, we believe, pretty generally abandoned. Such sentences as "Are you going to Vest Vickham?" "This is werry good weal," &c., were too intolerable to be retained. Moreover, there has been a very able schoolmaster at work during the past thirteen

years. This schoolmaster is no other than the loquacious *Mr. Punch*, from whose works we quote a few admirable exercises:–

1. *Low Cockney* – "Seen that party lately?" "What! the party with the wooden leg, as come with–" "No, no – not that party. The party, you know, as–" "Oh! Ah! I know the party you mean, now." "Well, a party told me as he can't agree with that other party, and he says that if another party can't be found to make it all square, he shall look out for a party as will." – (*And so on for half-an-hour.*)

2. *Police* – "Lor, Soosan, how's a feller to eat meat such weather as this? Now, a bit o' pickled salmon and cowcumber, or a lobster salid *might* do."

3. *Cockney Yachtsman* – (Example of affectation.) – Scene: the Regatta Ball. – "I say, Tom, what's that little craft with the black velvet flying at the fore, close under the lee scuppers of the man-of-war?" "Why, from her fore and aft rig, and the cut of her mainsail, I should say she's down from the port of London; but I'll signal the commodore to come and introduce us!"

4. *Omnibus Driver* – *Old Acquaintance*: "A've a drop, Bill?" *Driver*: "Why, yer see, Jim, this 'ere young hoss has only bin in 'arness once afore, and he's such a beggar to bolt, ten to one if I leave 'im he'll be a-runnin' hoff, and a smashin' into suthun. Howsoever – here – (*handing reins to a timid passenger*) – lay hold, sir, I'll chance it!"

5. *Coster-monger* (to extremely genteel person). – "I say, guv'ner, give us a hist with this 'ere bilin' o' greens!" (A large hamper of market stuff.)

6. *Genteel Cockney* (by the sea-side). – *Blanche*: "How grand, how solemn, dear Frederick, this is! I really think the ocean is more beautiful under this aspect than under any other!" – *Frederick*: "Hm – ah! Per-waps. By-the-way, Blanche – There's a fella shwimping. S'pose we ask him if he can get us some pwans for breakfast to-mowaw mawning?"

7. *Stuck-up Cockney* – (*Small Swell enters a tailor's shop.*) – "A— Brown, A— want some more coats!" *Snip*: "Yes, sir. Thank you, sir. How many would you please to want?" *Small Swell*: "A— let me see; A—ll have eight. A— no, I'll have nine; and look here! A— shall want some trousers." *Snip*: "Yes, sir, thank you, sir. How many would you like?" *Small Swell*: "A— I don't know exactly. S'pose we say twenty-four pairs; and look here! Show me some patterns that won't be worn by any snobs!"

8. *Cockney Flunkey* – (*Country Footman meekly enquires of London Footman*) – "Pray, sir, what do you think of our town? A nice place, ain't it?" *London Footman* (*condescendingly*): "Vell, Joseph, I likes your town well enough. It's clean; your streets are hairy; and you've lots of rewins. But I don't like your champagne, it's all gewsberry!"

9. *Cockney Cabby* (*politely*) – "Beg pardon, sir; please don't smoke in the keb, sir; Ladies do complain o' the 'bacca uncommon. Better let me smoke it for yer outside, sir!"

10. *Military Cockney* – Lieutenant Blazer (of the Plungers) – "Gwood gwacious! Here's a howible go! The Infantwy's going to gwow a moustache!" *Cornet Huffey* (*whose face is whiskerless.*) "Yaw don't mean that! Wall! there's only one alternative for us. We must shave!"

11. *Juvenile Low Cockney* – "Jack! Whereabouts is 'Amstid-am?" *Jack* – "Well, I can't say exackerly, but I know it's somewhere near 'Ampstid-'Eath!"

12. *Cockney Domestic* – *Servant girl*. "Well, mam – Heverythink considered, I'm afraid you von't suit me. I've always bin brought up genteel; and I could'nt go nowheres where there ain't no footman kep'."

Another – *Lady* – "Wish to leave! why I thought, Thompson, you were very comfortable with me!" (*Thompson, who is extremely refined.*) "Ho yes, mum! I don't find no fault with you, mum – nor yet with master – but the truth *his*, mum – the *hother* servants is so 'orrid vulgar and hignorant, and speaks so hungrammatical, that I reely cannot live in the same 'ouse with 'em – and I should like to go this day month, if so be has it won't illconvenience you!"

13. *Cockney Waiter* – "'Am Sir? Yessir? Don't take anything with your 'am, do you, sir?" *Gentleman* – "Yes, I do; I take the letter H!"

14. *Cockney Hairdresser* – "They say, sir, the cholera 'is in the Hair, sir!" *Gent* (*very uneasy*). – "Indeed! ahem! Then I hope you're very particular about the brushes you use." *Hairdresser* – "Oh, I see, you

don't *h*understand me, sir; I don't mean the 'air of the 'ed, but the *h*air *h*of the *h*atmosphere!"

15. *Cockney Sweep (seated upon a donkey)* – "Fitch us out another pen'north o' strawberry hice, with a dollop o' lemon water in it."

16. *Feminine Cockney (by the sea side.)* "Oh Harriette, dear, put on your hat and let us thee the stheamboat come in. The thea is tho rough! – and the people will be *tho* abthurdly thick!"

LONDONERS who desire to correct the defects of their utterance cannot do better than to exercise themselves frequently upon those words respecting which they have been in error.

HINTS FOR THE CORRECTION OF THE IRISH BROGUE – According to the directions given by Mr. B. H. Smart, an Irishman wishing to throw off the brogue of his mother country, should avoid hurling out his words with a superfluous quantity of breath. It is not *broadher* and *widher* that he should say, but the *d*, and every other consonant should be neatly delivered by the tongue, with as little riot, clattering, or breathing as possible. Next let him drop the roughness or rolling of the *r* in all places but the beginning of syllables: he must not say *stor-rum* and *far-rum*, but let the word be heard in one smooth syllable. He should exercise himself until he can convert *plaze* into *please*, *plinty* into *plenty*, *Jasus* into *Jesus*, and so on. He should modulate his sentences, so as to avoid directing his accent all in one manner – from the acute to the grave. Keeping his ear on the watch for good examples, and exercising himself frequently upon them, he may become master of a greatly improved utterance.

HINTS FOR CORRECTING THE SCOTCH BROGUE – The same authority remarks that as an Irishman uses the closing accent of the voice too much, so a Scotchman has the contrary habit, and is continually drawling his tones from the grave to the acute, with an effect which, to southern ears, is suspensive in character. The smooth gutteral *r* is as little heard in Scotland as in Ireland, the trilled *r* taking its place. The substitution of the former instead of the latter must be a matter of practice. The peculiar sound of the *u*, which in the north so often borders on the French *u*, must be compared with the several sounds of the letter as they are heard in the south; and the long quality which a Scotchman is apt to give to the vowels that ought to be essentially short, must be clipped. In fact, aural observation and lingual exercise are the only sure means to the end; so that a Scotchman going to a well for a bucket of water, and finding a countryman bathing therein, would not exclaim, "Hey, Colin, dinna ye ken the watter's for drink, and nae for bathin?"

OF PROVINCIAL BROGUES it is scarcely necessary to say much, as the foregoing advice applies to them. One militia man exclaimed to another, "Jim, you bain't in step." "Bain't I," exclaimed the other, "Well, change yourn!" Whoever desires knowledge must strive for it. It must not be dispensed with after the fashion of Tummus and Jim, who held the following dialogue upon a vital question:– *Tummus* – "I zay, Jim, be you a purtectionist?" *Jim* – "E'as I be." *Tummus* – "Wall I zay, Jim, what *be* purtection?" *Jim* – "Loa'r, Tummus, do'ant 'ee knaw?" *Tummus* – "Naw, I doan't." *Jim* – "Wall, I doan't knaw as I can tell 'ee, Tummus, *vur I doan't ezakerly knaw mysel'!*"

RULES OF PRONUNCIATION

C before *a*, *o*, and *u*, and in some other situations, is a close articulation, like *k*. Before *e i* and *y*, *c* is precisely equivalent to *s* in *same*, *this*, as in *cedar*, *civil*, *cypress*, *capacity*.

E final indicates that the preceding vowel is long, as in hate, mete, sire, robe, lyre, abate, recede, invite, remote, intrude.

E final indicates that *c* preceding has the sound of *s*, as in *lace*, *lance*; and that *g* preceding has the sound of j, as in *charge*, *page*, *challenge*.

E final, in proper English words, never forms a syllable, and in the most used words, in the terminating unaccented syllable, it is silent.

Thus, *motive, genuine, examine, juvenile, reptile, granite*, are pronounced *motiv, genuin, examin, juvenil, reptil, granit*.

E final, in a few words of foreign origin, forms a syllable, as *syncope, simile*.

E final is silent after *l* in the following terminations, *ble, cle, dle, fle, gle, kle, ple, tle, zle*; as in *able, manacle, cradle, ruffle, mangle, wrinkle, supple, rattle, puzzle*, which are pronounced *ab'l, man'acl, cra'dl, ruf'fl, man'gl, wrinkl, sup'pl, puz'zl*.

E is usually silent in the termination *en*, as in *token, broken*; pronounced *tokn, brokn*.

OUS in the termination of adjectives and their derivatives is pronounced *us*, as in *gracious, pious, pompously*.

CE, CI, TI, before a vowel, have the sound of *sh*; as in *cetaceous, gracious, motion, partial, ingratiate*, pronounced *cetashus, grachus, moshon, parshal, ingrashiate*.

TI, after a consonant, have the sound of *ch*, as in *Christian, bastion*; pronounced *Chrischan, baschan*.

SI, after an accented vowel, are pronounced like *zh*, as in *Ephesian, confusion*; pronounced *Ephezhan, confuzhan*.

When CI or IT precede similar combinations, as in pronun*ciati*on, nego*tiati*on, they may be pronounced *ce*, instead of *she*, to prevent a repetition of the latter syllable; as *pronunceashon*, instead of *pronunsheashon*.

GH, both in the middle and at the end of words are silent; as in *caught, bought, fright, nigh, sigh*; pronounced *caut, baut, frite, ni, si*. In the following exceptions, however, GH are pronounced as *F*: - *cough, chough, clough, enough, laugh, rough, slough, tough, trough*.

When WH begin a word, the aspirate *h* precedes *w* in pronunciation; as in *what, whiff, whale*; pronounced *hwat, hwiff, hwale, w* having precisely the sound of *oo*; French *ou*. In the following words *w* is silent: - *who, whom, whose, whoop, whole*.

H after *r* has no sound or use; as in *rheum, rhyme*; pronounced *reum, ryme*.

H should be sounded in the middle of words; as in fore*h*ead, ab*h*or, be*h*old, ex*h*aust, in*h*abit, un*h*orse.

H should always be sounded except in the following words: - heir, herb, honest, honour, hospital, hostler, hour, humour, and humble, and all their derivatives; – such as humorously, derived from humour.

K and G are silent before *n*; as *know, gnaw*; pronounced *no, naw*.

W before *r* is silent; as in *wring, wreath*; pronounced *ring, reath*.

B after *m* is silent; as in *dumb, numb*; pronounced *dum, num*.

L before *k* is silent; as in *baulk, walk, talk*; pronounced *bauk, wauk, tauk*.

PH have the sound of *f*; as in *philosophy*; pronounced *filisophy*.

NG has two sounds; one as in *singer* – the other as in *fin-ger*.

N after *m*, and closing a syllable, is silent, as in *hymn, condemn*.

P before *s* and *t* is mute, as in *psalm, pseudo, ptarmigan*; pronounced *sam, sudo, tarmigan*.

R has two sounds, one strong and vibrating, as at the beginning of words and syllables, such as *robber, reckon, error*; the other as at the terminations of words, or when it is succeeded by a consonant, as *farmer, morn*.

Before the letter R there is a slight sound of *e* between the vowel and the consonant. Thus, *bare, parent, apparent, mere, mire, more, pure, pyre*, are pronounced nearly *baer, paerent, appaerent, me-er, mier, moer, puer, pyer*. This pronunciation proceeds from the peculiar articulation *r*, and it occasions a slight change of the sound of *a*, which can only be learned by the ear.

PRONOUNCE
—ace, not iss, as furn*ace*, not furn*iss*.
—age, not idge, as cabb*age*, cour*age*, post*age*, vill*age*.
—ain, ane, not in, as cert*ain*, cert*ane*, not cert*in*.
—ate, not it, as moder*ate*, not moder*it*.
—ct, not c, as aspe*ct*, not aspe*c*; subje*ct*, not subje*c*.
 —ed, not id, or ud, as wick*ed*, not wick*id*, or wick*ud*.
—el, not l, mod*el*, not mod*l*; nov*el*, not nov*l*.
—en, not n, as sudd*en*, not sudd*n* – Burden, burthen, garden, lengthen, seven, strengthen, often, and a few others, have the *e* silent.
—ence, not *unce*, as influ*ence*, not influ-*unce*.
—es, not is, as pleas*es*, not pleas*is*.
—ile, should be pronounced il, as fert*il*, not fert*ile*, in all words except chamomile (*cam*), exile, gentile, infantile, reconcile, and senile, which should be pronounced īle.
—in, not n, as in Lat*in*, not Lat*n*.
—nd, not n, as husba*nd*, not husba*n*; thousa*nd*, not thousa*n*.
—ness, not n*iss*, as carefull*ness*, not carefuln*iss*.
—ng, not n, as singi*ng*, not singi*n*; speaki*ng*, not speaki*n*.
—ngth, not nth, as stre*ngth*, not stre*nth*.
—son, the *o* should be silent, as in treason, *tre-zn*, not *tre-son*.
—tal, not tle, as capi*tal*, not capi*tle*; me*tal*, not me*ttle*; mor*tal*, not mor*tle*; periodi*cal*, not periodi*cle*.
—xt, not x, as ne*xt*, not ne*x*.

PUNCTUATION – Punctuation teaches the method of placing *Points*, in written or printed matter, in such a manner as to indicate the pauses which would be made by the author if he were communicating his thoughts orally instead of by written signs.

WRITING AND PRINTING are substitutes for oral communication; and correct punctuation is essential to convey the meaning intended, and to give due force to such passages as the author may wish to impress upon the mind of the person to whom they are being communicated.

THE POINTS are as follows:–
The Comma ,
The Semicolon ;
The Colon :
The Period, or Full Point .
The Apostrophe '
The Hyphen, or Conjoiner -
The Note of Interrogation ?
The Note of Exclamation !
The Parenthesis ( )
The Asterisk, or Star *

AS THESE are all the points required in simple epistolary composition, we will confine our explanations to the rules which should govern the use of them.

BUT we will first state that the other points are the paragraph ¶; the section §; the dagger †; the rule —; the parallel ||; the bracket [ ]; and some others. These, however, are quite unnecessary, except for elaborate works, and in these they are chiefly used for notes or marginal references.

THE COMMA, denotes the shortest pause; the semicolon ; a little longer pause than the comma; the colon : a little longer pause than the semicolon; the period, or full-point . the longest pause.

THE RELATIVE DURATION of these pauses is described as–

While you count

Comma	One
Semicolon	Two
Colon	Three
Period	Four

This, however, is not an infallible rule, because the duration of the pauses should be regulated by the degree of rapidity with which the matter is being read. In slow reading, the duration of the pauses should be increased.

THE OTHER points are rather indications of expression, and of meaning and connection, than of pauses, and therefore we will notice them separately.

THE MISPLACING of even so slight a point, or pause, as the comma, will often alter the meaning of a sentence. The contract made for lighting the town of Liverpool, during the year 1819, was thrown void by the misplacing of a comma in the advertisements – thus:–
"The lamps at present are about 4050, and have in general two spouts each, composed of not less than twenty threads of cotton." The contractor would have proceeded to furnish each lamp with the said twenty threads; but this being but half the usual quantity, the commissioners discovered that the difference arose from the comma following instead of preceding the word *each*. The parties agreed to annul the contract, and a new one was ordered.

THE FOLLOWING sentence shows how difficult it is to read without the aid of the points used as pauses:–
Death waits not for storm or sunshine within a dwelling in one of the upper streets respectable in appearance and furnished with such conveniences as distinguish the habitations of those who rank among the higher classes of society a man of middle age lay on his last bed momently awaiting the final summons all that the most skilful

medical attendance all that love warm as the glow that fires an angel's bosom could do had been done by day and night for many long weeks had ministering spirits such as a devoted wife and loving children are done all within their power to ward off the blow but there he lay his raven hair smoothed off from his noble brow his dark eyes lighted with unnatural brightness and contrasting strongly with the pallid hue which marked him as an expectant of the dread messenger.

THE SAME sentence, properly pointed, and with capital letters placed after full points, according to the adopted rule, may be easily read and understood:–

Death waits not for storm or sunshine. Within a dwelling in one of the upper streets, respectable in appearance, and furnished with such conveniences as distinguish the habitations of those who rank among the higher classes of society, a man of middle age lay on his last bed, momently awaiting the final summons. All that the most skilful medical attendance – all that love, warm as the glow that fires an angel's bosom, could do, had been done; by day and night, for many long weeks, had ministering spirits, such as a devoted wife and loving children are, done all within their power to ward off the blow. But there he lay, his raven hair smoothed off from his noble brow, his dark eyes lighted with unnatural brightness, and contrasting strongly with the pallid hue which marked him as an expectant of the dread messenger.

THE APOSTROPHE ' is used to indicate the combining of two words in one – as John's book, instead of John, his book; or to show the omission of parts of words, as Glo'ster, for Gloucester – tho' for though. These abbreviations should be avoided as much as possible. Cobbett says the apostrophe "ought to be called the mark of *laziness* and *vulgarity*." The first use, however, of which we gave an example, is a necessary and proper one.

THE HYPHEN or conjoiner - is used to unite words which, though they are separate and distinct, have so close a connection as almost to become one word, as water-rat, wind-mill, &c. It is also used in writing and printing, at the end of a line, to show where a word is divided and continued in the next line. Look down the ends of the lines in this column, and you will notice the hyphen in several places.

THE NOTE OF INTERROGATION ? indicates that the sentence to which it is put asks a question, as "What is the meaning of that assertion? What am I to do?"

THE NOTE OF EXCLAMATION or of admiration ! indicates surprise, pleasure, or sorrow, as "Oh! Ah! Goodness! Beautiful! I am astonished! Woe is me!"

THE PARENTHESIS ( ) is used to prevent confusion by the introduction to a sentence, of a passage not necessary to the sense thereof. "I am going to meet Mr. Smith (though I am no admirer of him) on Wednesday next." It is better, however, as a rule, not to employ parenthetical sentences.

THE ASTERISK or star * may be employed to refer from the text to a note of explanation at the foot of a column, or at the end of a letter. *** Three stars are sometimes used to call particular attention to a paragraph.

HINTS UPON SPELLING – The following rules will be found of great assistance in writing, because they relate to a class of words about the spelling of which doubt and hesitation are frequently felt:–

All words of one syllable ending in *l*, with a single vowel before it, have double *l* at the close: as, *mill*, *sell*.

All words of one syllable ending in *l*, with a double vowel before it, have one *l* only at the close; as *mail*, *sail*.

Words of one syllable ending in *l*, when compounded, retain but one *l* each; as, *fulfil*, *skilful*.

Words of more than one syllable ending in *l* have one *l* only at the close; as, *delightful*, *faithful*; except *befall*, *downfall*, *recall*, *unwell*, &c.

All derivations from words ending in *l* have one *l* only; as *equality*, from *equal*; *fulness*, from *full*; except they end in *er* or *ly*; as *mill*, *miller*; *full*, *fully*.

All participles in *ing* from verbs ending in *e* lose the *e* final; as *have, having*; *amuse, amusing*; unless they come from verbs ending in double *e*, and then they retain both; as, *see, seeing*; *agree, agreeing*.

All adverbs in *ly* and nouns in *ment* retain the *e* final of the primitives; as, *brave, bravely*; *refine, refinement*; except *acknowledgment* and *judgment*.

All derivations from words ending in *er* retain the *e* before the *r*; as, *refer, reference*; except *hindrance*, from *hinder*; *remembrance* from *remember*; *disastrous*, from *disaster*; *monstrous*, from *monster*; *wondrous* from *wonder*; *cumbrous* from *cumber*, &c.

Compound words, if both end not in *l*, retain their primitive parts entire; as, *millstone, changeable, raceless*; except *always, also, deplorable, although, almost, admirable*, &c.

All one-syllables ending in a consonant, with a single vowel before it, double that consonant in derivatives; as, *sin, sinner*; *ship, shipping*; *big, bigger*; *glad, gladder*, &c.

One-syllables ending in a consonant, with a double vowel before it, do not double the consonant in derivatives; as, *sleep, sleepy*; *troop, trooper*.

All words of more than one syllable ending in a single consonant, preceded by a single vowel, and accented on the last syllable, double that consonant in derivatives; as *commit, committee*; *compel, compelled*; *appal, appalling*; *distil, distiller*.

Nouns of one syllable ending in *y*, preceded by a consonant, change *y* into *ies* in the plural; and verbs ending in *y*, preceded by a consonant, change *y* into *ies* in the third person singular of the present tense, and into *ied* in the past tense and past participle; as, *fly*, *flies*; *I apply*, *he applies*; *we reply*, *we replied* or *have replied*. If the *y* be preceded by a vowel, this rule is not applicable; as, *key*, *keys*; *I play*, *he plays*; we have *enjoyed* ourselves.

Compound words whose primitives end in *y* change *y* into *i*; as *beauty*, *beautiful*; *lovely*, *loveliness*.

H OR NO H? THAT IS THE QUESTION – Few things point so directly to the want of *cultivation* as the misuse of the letter H by persons in conversation. We hesitate to assert that this common defect in speaking indicates the absence of *education* – for, to our surprise, we have heard even educated persons frequently commit this common and vulgar error. Now, for the purpose of assisting those who desire to improve their mode of speaking, we intend to tell a little story about our next door neighbour, Mrs. Alexander Hitching, – or, as she frequently styled herself, with an air of conscious dignity, Mrs. *Halexander 'Itching*. Her husband was a post captain of some distinction, seldom at home, and therefore Mrs. A. H. (or, as she rendered it, Mrs. *H. I.*) felt it incumbent upon herself to represent her own dignity, and the dignity of her husband also. Well, this Mrs. Hitching was a next door neighbour of ours – a most agreeable lady in many respects, middle aged, good looking, uncommonly fond of talking, of active, almost of fussy habits, very good tempered and good natured, but with a most unpleasant habit of misusing the letter H to such a degree that our sensitive nerves have often been shocked when in her society. But we must beg the reader, if Mrs. H. should be an acquaintance of his, not to breathe a word of our having written this account of her – or there would be no limit to her "*h*indignation." And, as her family is very numerous, it will be necessary to keep the matter as quiet as can be, for it will scarcely be possible to mention the subject anywhere, without "*o*rrifying" some of her relations, and instigating them to make Mrs. H. become our "*h*enemy," instead of remaining, as we wish her to do, our intimate friend.

One morning Mrs. H. called upon me, and asked me to take a walk, saying that it was her *h*object to look out for an 'ouse, as her lease had nearly terminated; and as she had often heard her dear 'Itching say that he would like to settle in the neighbourhood of 'Ampstead 'Eath, she should like me to assist her by my judgment in the choice of a residence.

"I shall be most happy to accompany you," I said.

"I knew you would," said she: 'and I am sure a *h*our or two in your society will give me pleasure. It's so long since we've had a gossip. Besides which, I want a change of *h*air."

I glanced at her peruke, and for a moment laboured under the idea that she intended to call at her hairdresser's; but I soon recollected.

"I suppose we had better take the *h*omnibus," she remarked, "and we can get out at the foot of the 'ill."

I assented, and in a few minutes we were in the street; in the line of the omnibus, and one of those vehicles soon appearing–

"Will you 'ail it?" inquired she.

So I hailed it at once, and we got in. Now Mrs. H. was so fond of talking that the presence of strangers never restrained her – a fact which I have often had occasion to regret. She was no sooner within the omnibus than she begun remarking upon the *h*inconvenience of such vehicles, because of their smallness, and the *h*insolence of many of the conductors. She thought that the proprietors ought only to 'ire men upon whose civility they could depend. Then she launched out into larger topics – said she thought that the *H*emperor of *H*austria – (here I endeavoured to interrupt her by asking whether she had any idea of the part of Hampstead she would like; but she would complete her remarks by saying) – must be as 'appy as the days are long, now that the *H*empress had presented him with a *hare* to the throne! (Some of the passengers smiled, and, turning round, looked out of the windows.)

I much wished for our arrival at the spot where we should alight, for she commenced a story about a 'andsome young nephew of hers, who was a distinguished *h*officer in the *h*army. This was suggested to her, no doubt, by the presence in the omnibus of a fine looking young fellow, with a moustache. She said that at present her nephew was stationed in *H*ireland; but he expected soon to be *h*ordered to the Crimea.

The gentleman with the moustache seemed much amused, and smilingly asked her whether her nephew was at all *h*ambitious? I saw that he (the gentleman with the moustache) was jesting, and I would have given anything to have been released from the unpleasant predicament I was in. But what was my annoyance when Mrs. H. proceeded to say to this youth, whose face was radiant with humour, that it was the 'ight of her nephew's *h*ambition to serve his country in the *h*our of need; and then she proceeded to ask her fellow-traveller his opinion of the *h*upshot of the war – remarking that she 'oped it would soon be *h*over!

At this moment I felt so nervous that I pulled out my handkerchief, and endeavoured to create a diversion by making a loud nasal noise, and remarking that I thought the wind very cold, when an accident happened which took us all by surprise: one of the large wheels of the omnibus dropped off, and all the passengers were jostled down into a corner; but, fortunately, without serious injury. Mrs. H., however, happening to be under three or four persons, raised a loud cry for "'elp! 'elp!" She was speedily got out, when she assured us that she was not 'urt; but she was in such a state of *h*agitation that she wished to be taken to a chemist's shop, to get some *H*aromatic vinegar, or some *Hoe* de Cologne! The chemist was exceedingly polite to her, for which she said she could never express her *h*obligations – an assertion which seemed to me to be literally true.

She was some time before she resumed her accustomed freedom of conversation; but as we ascended the hill she explained to me that she should like to take the house as tenant from *'ear* to *'ear*! – but she thought landlords would *h*object to such an agreement, as when they got a good tenant they liked to 'old 'im as long as they could. She expressed an opinion that 'Ampstead must be very 'ealthy, because it was so 'igh *h*up.

We soon reached the summit of the hill, and turned through a lane which led towards the Heath, and in which villas and cottages were smiling on either side. "Now, there's a *h*elegant little place!" she exclaimed, "just suited to my *h*ideas – about *h*eight rooms, and a *h*oriel *h*over the *h*entrance." But it was not to let – so we passed on.

Presently, she saw something likely to suit her, and as there was a bill in the window, "To be Let – Inquire Within," she gave a 'lout rat-a-tat-tat at the door.

The servant opened it.

"I see that this 'ouse is to let?"

"Yes, ma'am it is; will you walk in?"

"'Ow many rooms are there?"

"Eleven, ma'am; but if you will step in, mistress will speak to you."

A very graceful lady made her appearance at the parlour door, and invited us to step in. I felt exceedingly nervous, for I at once perceived that the lady of the house spoke with that accuracy and taste which is one of the best indications of refinement.

"The house *is* to let – and a very pleasant residence we have found it."

"'Ave you *h*occupied it long?"

"Our family has resided here for more than nine years."

"Then, I suppose, your lease 'as run *h*out!"

"No! we have it for five years longer; but my brother, who is a clergyman, has been appointed to a living in Yorkshire, and for his sake, and for the pleasure of his society, we desire to remove."

"Well – there's nothing like keeping families together for the sake of 'appiness. Now, there's my poor dear 'Itching" – [here she paused, as if somewhat affected, and some young ladies who were in the room drew their heads together, and appeared to consult about their needlework; but I saw, by dimples upon their cheeks, which they could not conceal, that they were smiling] – "'e's 'itherto been *h*at 'ome so seldom, that I've 'ardly *h*ever known what 'appiness *h*is."

I somewhat abruptly broke in upon the conversation, by suggesting that she had better look through the house, and inquire the conditions of tenancy. We consequently went through the various rooms, and in every one of them she had "an *h*objection to this," or "a 'atred for that," or would give "a 'int which might be useful" to the lady when she removed. The young ladies were heard tittering very much as we walked across the staircases, for it generally happened upon these occasions that Mrs. H. broke out, in a loud voice, with her imperfect elocution. I felt so much annoyed, that I determined to cure Mrs. H. of her defective speaking.

RULES OF CONDUCT – We cannot do better than quote the valuable injunctions of that excellent woman, Mrs. Fry, who combined in her character and conduct all that is truly excellent in woman:–

1. I never lose any time; I do not think that lost which is spent in amusement or recreation some time every day; but always be in the habit of being employed. 2. Never err the least in truth. 3. Never say an ill thing of a person when thou canst say a good thing of him; not only speak charitably, but feel so. 4. Never be irritable or unkind to anybody. 5. Never indulge thyself in luxuries that are not necessary. 6. Do all things with consideration; and, when thy path to act right is most difficult, feel confidence in that Power alone which is able to assist thee, and exert thy own powers as far as they go.

GOSSIPING – If you wish to cultivate a gossiping, meddling, censorious spirit in your children, be sure when they come home from church, a visit, or any other place where you do not accompany them, to ply them with questions concerning what everybody wore, how everybody looked, and what everybody said and did; and if you find anything in this to censure, always do it in their hearing. You may rest assured, if you pursue a course of this kind, they will not return to you unlade with intelligence; and, rather than it should be uninteresting, they will by degrees learn to embellish, in such a manner as shall not fail to call forth remarks and expressions of wonder from you. You will, by this course, render the spirit of curiosity, which is so early visible in children, and which, if rightly directed, may be made the instrument of enriching and enlarging their minds – a vehicle of mischief which shall serve only to narrow them.

WORDS – Soft words soften the soul. Angry words are fuel to the flame of wrath, and make it blaze more freely. Kind words make other people good-natured. Cold words freeze people, and hot words scorch them, and bitter words make them bitter, and wrathful words make wrathful. There is such a rush of all other kinds of words in our days, that it seems desirable to give kind words a chance among them. There are vain words, and idle words, and hasty words, and spiteful words, and silly words, and empty words, and profane words, and boisterous words, and warlike words. Kind words also produce their own image on men's souls, and a beautiful image it is. They smooth, and quiet, and comfort the hearer. They shame him out of his sour, and morose, and unkind feelings. We have not yet begun to use kind words in such abundance as they ought to be used.

ADVICE TO YOUNG LADIES

If you have blue eyes you need not languish.

If black eyes you need not stare.

If you have pretty feet there is no occasion to wear short petticoats.

If you are doubtful as to that point, there can be no harm in letting them be long.

If you have good teeth, do not laugh for the purpose of showing them.

If you have bad ones, do not laugh less than the occasion may justify.

If you have pretty hands and arms, there can be no objection to your playing on the harp if you play well.

If they are disposed to be clumsy, work tapestry.

If you have a bad voice rather speak in a low tone.

If you have the finest voice in the world, never speak in a high tone.

If you dance well, dance but seldom.

If you dance ill, never dance at all.

If you sing well, make no previous excuses.

If you sing indifferently, hesitate not a moment when you are asked, for few people are judges of singing, but every one is sensible of a desire to please.

If you would preserve beauty, rise early.

If you would preserve esteem, be gentle.

If you would obtain power, be condescending.

If you would live happy, endeavour to promote the happiness of others.

Index